BAKING WITH LESS SUGAR

Joanne Chang *of* Flour Bakery + Café

BAKING WITH LESS SUGAR

RECIPES FOR DESSERTS *using*
NATURAL SWEETENERS *and*
LITTLE-TO-NO WHITE SUGAR

Photographs by Joseph De Leo

CHRONICLE BOOKS
SAN FRANCISCO

Library of Congress Cataloging-in-Publication Data available.

ISBN 978-1-4521-3300-3

Manufactured in China

Designed by Alice Chau

Food styling by Molly Shuster

10 9 8 7 6 5 4 3

Chronicle Books LLC
680 Second Street
San Francisco, California 94107
www.chroniclebooks.com

To Christopher, my everything.

CONTENTS

CHAPTER FOUR
BAKING WITH MAPLE SYRUP AND MOLASSES 123

CHAPTER FIVE
FRUIT IS SWEET 155

INTRODUCTION

Life is sweet. It is. It's not always easy. It's not without ups and downs, triumphs and tragedies. But LIFE *IS* SWEET. Why do I make this declaration? Because I've taken these simple words, swallowed them whole, and used them as words to live by. For as long as I can remember, no matter what my mood or what I'm feeling, it only takes a bite of something wonderful and sweet to make all seem right in the world. Baking is my life and I choose it every day as my path and my passion. On some level, my life is simply that simple.

Every morning, I walk into Flour and I stop for a moment to take in the full breadth of our morning bake-off. It's fourteen years and running, and it still makes me giddy at how gorgeous a full counter of beautifully prepared baked goods can be. It never gets old. I look around and I truly want to eat *all* of it. The counter is overrun with warm brioche neatly arranged on serving trays, sugary fruity muffins piled high in baskets, chewy oversized cookies lined up on platters, comforting quick breads stacked one on top of another. I look to the bakers and see the most lovely faces—focused, serious, committed, sometimes silly, sometimes exhausted—and I think Willy Wonka is alive and well at Flour Bakery. I'm happy.

Maybe the complexities of life can't all be reduced to a cookie . . . but a well-made cookie can sure bring some music into it. For me, the connection between baking sweets and happiness runs long and strong and it is indelible. If you're holding this book, then that connection—sweetness and happiness—more than likely is a powerful one for you as well. Whether you start the day with coffee

and a brioche, or reward yourself for making it through three-quarters of your work day with a cookie or half cupcake, or maybe you commemorate a friend's new venture with a gussied-up and decadent midnight chocolate cake—each of these situations shows how naturally we intertwine sweetness and happiness. Even in sorrow we might take refuge in a bowl (okay, pint) of Häagen-Dazs coffee. Sometimes the sweetness of that ice cream is exactly what it takes to wait out that agonizing soon-to-be ex's %#^$ phone call.

I am and always have been so committed to the notion that bringing sweetness into the world simply makes life better that I have made it my life's work. I had a more-than-stable and respectable job in business consulting. I traded it in to peddle pastry and desserts. NOT what you do when your parents immigrate to America, work their tails off to give you the best education on the planet, scrimp and save and sacrifice. No matter what I tried to focus on or what my parents subtly—or not so subtly—suggested (be a doctor, be a lawyer, what about medicine? what about law?), my dreams persistently ran to mounds of butter, mountains of flour, and ultimately, hills of sugar: the glorious trifecta of baked goods. It's such a part of my DNA to indulge in sweetness from the moment I wake up until I fall asleep that I made it my bakery's motto: Make Life Sweeter, Eat Dessert First!

A connection that runs just as deeply as that between sweetness and happiness is the relationship between sugar and sweetness. And, by the transitive property, then sugar must be the sine qua non of creating happiness, right? Well if you're a classically trained pastry chef, then yes. Absolutely. Of course. Or at least so I thought.

Over the last two decades as my experience as a pastry chef has grown, the one immutable lesson I am certain of is: The more I know the more I don't know. Every time I learn of a new ingredient or technique the boundaries of what I think makes an excellent pastry expand. Of course, molecular gastronomy—making mango foams and coffee air and caramel smoke and such—has introduced us all to flavors and textures never before seen in desserts until recently. But even less dramatic than that is realizing that nothing is absolute, especially what defines "delicious" to me. A recipe for chocolate mousse that I made when I was first starting out in pastry now tastes awfully bland to me; an almond torte that I used to swoon over, I barely cast a second glance at; ricotta turnovers that I couldn't wait to remove from the first pastry menu I inherited, I now adore. My previously unexamined assumption that sugar is the most direct source to creating the sweetness that we love has been tested over and over again as I've sampled and experimented with other far more interesting paths towards that same goal.

I've realized that desserts benefit from spanning the sweetener spectrum to include honey, maple, fruit juice, and more. I've surrounded myself with more and more ways of eating sweets all day long but in a more balanced fashion. I still crave something sweet as soon as I wake up . . . but it no longer needs to be covered in icing and showered in sugar. I have always believed that the best desserts highlight flavors other than just that of sweet, sweet, sweet. Nuts and fruits and cream and chocolate are all such enticing flavors, and they should be the stars of the show. My own personal favorite pastries are those that showcase the richness of creamy butter, the round warmth of vanilla bean,

the balance of acid and sweetness in fresh fruit, the spiciness of grated nutmeg, in fact everything but the hit-over-your-head aspect of sugary sweet flavors that I used to crave.

The running joke in the Chang-Myers household is that, despite the fact that all I eat all day long is cake and cookies and muffins, we have nary a pastry in the house. It didn't start out that way. In fact, part of the wooing process Christopher went through when we were first dating was to visit me at the first Flour almost every single day to get his morning pastry and/or afternoon treat. His sweet tooth rivals mine (it is one of the many, many ways I knew immediately he was the one for me), and over a slice of carrot cake or a shared chocolate cupcake we would banter and joke and flirt. Was he here to see me or because he was addicted to our peanut butter cookies and lemon tarts? Or both? Now that we are married he teases me that I pulled the wool over his eyes. He thought he signed up for a lifetime supply of baked goods, but day in and day out I come home empty-handed. "We're like the shoemaker's children who never have shoes!" he declares. "We never have sweets in the house!"

As life would have it, it turns out that Christopher is sensitive to sugar. It fills him up with giddy energy and then sends him crashing down into a daze. I've witnessed the sugar rush and ensuing inevitable crash enough times to finally see the pattern. How ironic is it that sugar—the stalwart ingredient of my career—is the culprit? Over the years I've searched for other ways to satisfy his sugar cravings, starting with simple fruit treats like frozen bananas dipped in bittersweet chocolate, and mango sorbets made creamy with a hit of coconut milk to more involved pastries like a sticky toffee pudding cake sweetened with just a touch of maple syrup, and granola bars full of dried fruit and bound together with a smidge of honey. I am fascinated by the exploration of finding other ways to add flavor and delight to a dessert without relying on white sugar. And I know you will be, too.

Here you will learn to bake all of your favorite pastries with minimal or no refined white sugar. While sugar is obviously the most common sweetener used in baking, it's by no means your only option. You will discover, as I did, that when you don't focus on sugar and sweetness, you end up with desserts that are full of amazing, compelling flavor. Many sugar alternatives are items you already have stocked in your pantry. You will incorporate sweetness into desserts with more varied ingredients such as honey, maple syrup, chocolate, and fruit. White sugar is familiar and pleasing, but these alternate sources of sweetness offer more alluring, complex flavors and deeper, more interesting elements to your desserts in ways that sugar alone can't.

You'll find recipes for White Chocolate–Cherry–Almond Cookies (page 47), Yellow Birthday Cake with Fluffy Chocolate Ganache Frosting (page 62), and Cinnamon Sugar Monkey Bread (page 37) that you and your family will clamor for . . . made with a fraction of the white sugar that these treats typically use. You will bake Banana Cinnamon Bread Pudding (page 103) sweetened only with honey and a Pear-Maple Tarte Tatin (page 147) that relies on maple syrup, not sugar, for sweetness. A decadent Truffle Chocolate Cream Pie (page 88) is made with no added sugar other than the sugar that is in the chocolate, and it will become your new favorite dessert to satisfy the chocoholics in your life. You won't believe that Carrot-Pineapple Cake with Cream Cheese Frosting (page 186) and buttery flaky Spiced Pear Turnovers (page 161) have no white sugar, and you'll learn how to sweeten desserts with simply fruit and fruit juices. You will be amazed over and over at how you can make awesome baked goods that contain little to no white sugar. You will realize that you can bake with less or no sugar for exactly the same reason why we bake in general: to make fabulous, scrumptious desserts that you, your friends, and your family love to eat.

WHY LOW/ NO SUGAR?

I sell sugar. Plain and simple, it's what I do. The hallmark of every beloved pastry is that it is SWEET. That's what makes it dessert! In fact my first book, *Flour*, is a celebration of all of the magical delights you can create when sugar is the star. So what in the world am I doing making pastries that have little or even no sugar? It wasn't something that came to me automatically. My goal in baking has always been to bake something that is so mouthwatering you simply can't stop eating it when you try it. We look to our refrigerators and pantries for inspiration and then guided by a taste memory or a new idea, we create ooey-gooey, fluffy, tender, delectable treats. When testing recipes for the bakery, when we make something that I end up gobbling down in one sitting and looking around for more, then I know we've hit on something good. Pretty much the only restriction I've had to figure out so far is, how do we make space on our pastry counter to showcase this must-have dessert?

A few years ago, I read an article in the *New York Times* titled, "Is Sugar Toxic?" by Gary Taubes that questioned whether or not we as a nation were consuming too much sugar. It reminded me of when I was first opening up Flour about a decade earlier and was faced with dealing with the low-carb movement and Atkins diet acolytes. Who was going to come to a place called Flour when it was being branded the enemy? It's so easy to fall into the trap of changing our eating—and thus our cooking and baking—based on the latest trendy research. (Eggs are good! Eggs are bad! Now they

are good again!). I've done it myself over the years—anyone else remember sprinkling oat bran on everything we ate and making muffins and pancakes with it? *Not this again!* I thought to myself.

But yes, this again. When the article came out, I was finishing up my second book, *Flour, Too*, and looking forward to new challenges. I'd been bitten by the cookbook-writing bug (when it gets in you, it's hard to escape), and I was toying with a few different cookbook ideas in my head. Should I do a Myers+Chang book (it's in the works!), or maybe a "how to open a bakery business" book, or follow the trends and work on a gluten-free or maybe a vegan baking book? Out of the blue, my editors at Chronicle Books called me and asked what I thought about writing a low-sugar baking book. I'd dabbled a bit in some low-sugar baking at home; Christopher tries to balance his white sugar intake when he can, which can be difficult when your wife is a pastry chef. But I'd never actively thought about compiling a list of recipes with little to no sugar. "Think about it!" they urged me and we hung up the phones. Not a week later *O Magazine*—yes, *that* O—contacted me and asked me if I had any interest in contributing to an article they were writing on no-sugar desserts. I almost thought it must be a joke. (Or those folks at Chronicle were pulling out all the stops to get me to consider their idea!!) Turns out *O Magazine* was simply ahead of the curve, and they wanted to see what I could do without any white sugar. The seed was planted.

I contributed a few recipes to the article, fell in love with how mouthwateringly delicious they were (as did Christopher), and continued to be intrigued with the idea of developing dessert recipes that rivaled those of my first and second cookbooks that were made with little to no refined white sugar. Could I create pastries that would fully gratify our incessant sugar cravings while still pleasing parents, doctors, health addicts, and anyone else wanting to reduce the amount of sugar we consume each day? Every single moment at work I'm surrounded by sugar. How easy or hard would it be to teach people's taste buds to enjoy desserts that are not over the top with sweetness? A hallmark of many of the desserts we sell at the bakery is that they are not crazy sweet; sure, we have some pastries that are pretty decadent, but the majority of our treats are already well balanced in the sweetness department. How far could I continue this trend? I made a low-sugar oatmeal raisin cookie and a low-sugar banana bread just to see what the result would be . . . and I was hooked! My bakers and I all loved the newer versions of these Flour classics so much that I immediately imagined creating a new baking book, one that carried on the same "I can't stop eating this" philosophy with recipes that had a fraction of the sugar, if any at all, in them.

I'm no doctor (to the chagrin of my mom, who comes from a family of doctors), so in no way is this book a medical treatise on how to eat better or a diatribe against sugars. Nor is it a diabetic or no-sugar baking book by any means. As an active member of the food community known for providing baked goods made with real whole ingredients, I saw a unique challenge to create sweet treats that people love that are less dependent on sugar than their traditional counterparts and that use other sweeteners to taste delicious. One of my cookbook readers even reached out to say, "Since I've started baking, I am surprised by the amount of sugar stated in cookbooks, and I wonder, do people really eat that much sugar and does the recipe need that much sugar. I have a sweet tooth but not that sweet a tooth. I am not a health nut. I just feel one does not depend solely on sugar to make baking delicious." Mandy in Singapore, I couldn't have said it better myself.

Working in the food business, I've become aware of all of the variations of abstinence eating: some of us shy away from fat or carbs for health purposes, others might avoid nuts or dairy for allergy reasons, still others abstain from animal products or meats out of personal preference. I will never not eat sugar—it's programmed w-a-a-a-ay too much into my life. We can still have our cake and eat it too if we learn to satisfy our cravings in other ways. These recipes are for every one of us. So here is a baking book, using my experience in the pastry kitchen and my knowledge of the science of baking, to help you change your palate to appreciate less-sweet pastries as well as employ alternate sweeteners in your baking to satisfy your sweet tooth.

So back to the question at hand . . . what made me tackle low/no sugar baking? Well, for starters, there are our customers. At Flour, we are happily entrenched in the neighborhoods we have established ourselves in. We get to know our regulars, and our goal each and every day is to try and make our guests' days with our smiles and delicious food. Every pastry and sandwich and coffee has to pass the Mom Test—would you hand this to your mother and be proud of it?—and if it doesn't, we won't serve it. When we opened the first Flour, I worked hard on making a menu that everyone would love. I tried to pack it with home-run favorites, special twists on classics, interesting takes on the most popular pastries, and it took off. We've listened to our guests over the years, adding things, changing things, and adjusting ourselves so that we are continuing to offer what they want. It's not easy when you are trying to please everyone! But I think we've hit on a nice balance of making many, many people happy with our food. Over the years, we've had requests for gluten-free foods, nut-free selections, and vegan and vegetarian options. All of these have been incorporated into our menu, and we are always on the hunt for how we can improve. More and more guests are reaching out asking if we can create the same desserts they know, crave, and love with less sugar. What I've noticed is that these requests come from everyone: women and men, young and old, parents and singles. Choosing to consume less refined sugar is not a diet issue that pushes different groups' buttons. Rather, it is the approach that always wins the day for all of us: intention and moderation over restriction and elimination.

Besides responding to the requests of our guests, doctor or not, I am aware of the over-consumption we as a nation have of sugar and the numerous health implications. A decade ago I'd never heard the term *glycemic index*. Now it is the catchphrase of the day. Different foods are assigned a GI rating based on how they cause our blood sugar to rise when we consume them. The higher the GI, the more rapid the rise in blood sugar. When you consume foods that cause your blood sugar to rise and fall, your body sometimes has trouble with the spikes and valleys. As a result you could develop insulin resistance, which has been linked to everything from diabetes to obesity to heart disease. Whoa! For those looking to continue to indulge in baking but be intentional about their sugar intake, I want to share the other ways in which I've learned to satisfy my sweet tooth.

My dad taught me, "Everything in moderation," and I try mightily to follow his lead. If I deprive myself of something, especially if it is something that I love, it becomes unbearably appealing— more so than if I had just indulged in a little in the first place. But I know how easy it is to chuck moderation out the window when faced with a tempting treat. As much as I like to preach, "Just take a little! Don't eat the whole thing!" I know that is easier said than done. By minimizing the amount of sweeteners in these pastries, some of the moderating is already done. As someone who pretty much eats only pastries for most of the day, it is a goal of mine to be able to continue to indulge in all of my favorite foods while addressing the issue of too much sugar in my system. I've witnessed firsthand that once you learn to rein in your sugar intake, your palate adjusts to desserts that are not super-sweet, and you end up enjoying these treats much more.

Finally, the best reason for me to create these low-sugar recipes is that they are simply delicious and it was incredibly fun! In 2007, when I was challenged by Bobby Flay in *Throwdown with Bobby Flay*, it was initially set up as a ruse in which I was filming *The Science of Sweets* (see What's Behind the Science of Sweets, page 17). I'm fascinated by the alchemy and magic—I guess that's chemistry!— of how the various ingredients in baking all come together to form something so much more than the sum of their parts. Baking with little to no sugar is an extension of that passion. Could I bake desserts and pastries that pass my "can't stop eating it" test but have less sugar? *How* could I do it? What changes would result? Was it just about tricking the palate to adjust to less sugar, or was it possible to simply become accustomed to less-sweet desserts? I've never had as many joys—and crushing failures—in testing recipes as I did here. I've learned so much more than I ever expected and even though this book is done, I'm continuing my quest to give my favorite desserts the low-sugar treatment.

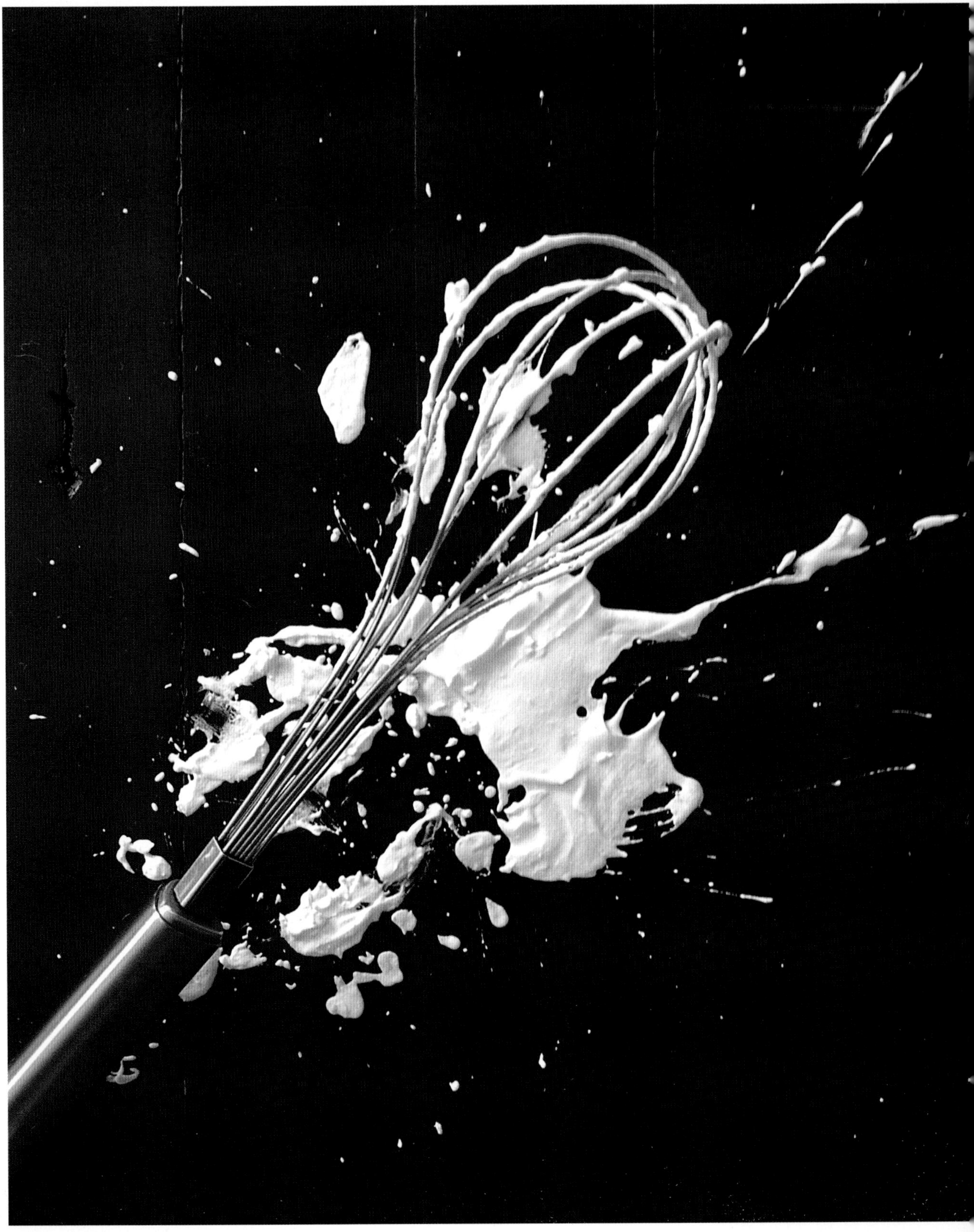

WHAT IS LOW/NO SUGAR?

When baking, I am pretty laser focused on one thing—creating pastries that are simply irresistible—and these recipes are no exception. In defining "low sugar" I took a moderate approach, so if you are aiming to reduce the amount of refined white sugar you are baking with, these recipes will help you learn to do so. The working definition for "low sugar" varies by chapter.

In the first chapter, we simply bake with less sugar. Standard recipes like our decadent chocolate brownies get the "low-sugar" treatment, and most recipes contain 100 g/½ cup of sugar or less with just a few at more than 165 g/⅔ cup. All of these desserts have at least half the amount of sugar of their full-sugar counterparts. They are not diabetic nor ascetically non-sweet. Instead, they are an introduction to how you can make pastries that still have that WOW! factor while knowing that they contain significantly less sugar than is typical.

Next, we delve into desserts made with bitter-sweet chocolate. All chocolate, except unsweet-ened chocolate and cocoa powder, is made with sugar, and you can use that to your advantage to decrease the amount of added sugar in your desserts. These recipes rely on just chocolate as the sweetener for truly indulgent treats, with no additional sugar, allowing you to continue your journey in baking with less sugar. I use a fruity bittersweet chocolate that has a cacao percentage of 68 percent. This means that 68 percent of the chocolate is pure cacao, and the remaining

32 percent is sugar, cocoa butter, and flavorings like vanilla. For each ounce of this chocolate there are approximately 11 grams of sugar, which trans-lates to about 2½ teaspoons of sugar. I indicate in each recipe the total amount of sugar that comes from the sugar within the chocolate so you can have an idea of how much refined white sugar is in these recipes. Some of the recipes in this chapter use this to full advantage, and the resulting des-serts are as rich and decadent as can be. Others skirt the line between sweet enough to just barely sweet; true chocolate aficionados who revel in the flavors of cacao will appreciate these desserts.

Honey as a sweetener headlines the next group of desserts and pastries. Honey has been naturally sweetening desserts for centuries; these recipes often have an old-fashioned and exotic flavor to me, since I grew up really only tasting honey when someone's grandma made a honey cake or when traveling in the Mediterranean where honey desserts are quite common. These recipes use anywhere from 115 g/¼ cup to 225 g/⅔ cup of honey, with the last two recipes topping out at 340 g/1 cup honey total between cake and frosting.

Next is the chapter on desserts made with maple syrup or molasses or both. Maple syrup is sap that is tapped directly from maple trees in the spring; it lends a gentle, buttery sweetness when used in baking. Molasses is the by-product of the refining of cane or beet sugar and has a strong, sharp flavor that works best in old-fashioned cakes and puddings. Both have distinctive, delightful flavors that make dreamy no-sugar desserts. Instead of white sugar, we rely on around 160 g/½ cup to 240 g/¾ cup of maple syrup or molasses in the recipes in this chapter, with a few at 320 g/1 cup of total syrup or molasses. It's easy to overdo the sweetness when working with maple syrup because of how pleasing it is, so I created desserts that use maple syrup to highlight other flavors like pears, cranberries, and pumpkin. Molasses is much more potent—a little goes a long way—so we use it sparingly for its spicy punch.

We end with fruit, both fresh fruits and fruit juices. Naturally sweetening your desserts with fruit allows you to avoid white sugar while still creating nostalgic, tantalizing baked goods that no one would guess are sugar-free. I've been a fruit freak my whole life. Despite the fact that I'm surrounded by sugary pastries all day long, my go-to snack is always a piece of fresh fruit. The desserts in here are among my favorite since they allow me to highlight all of the intensely flavorful and wonderful aspects of different kinds of fruit, from dried to fresh to reduced juices.

WHAT'S BEHIND THE SCIENCE OF SWEETS?

In 2007, the Food Network contacted me and asked if I would help them by filming the pilot episode of a new series they were starting called *The Science of Sweets*. Would I?! I jumped at the chance to share my passion on how baking is chemistry. I am awed daily by the transformation that occurs each time you mix together butter and sugar and flour and eggs and create something so utterly different than what you start out with. It turns out that the whole Science of Sweets idea was a ruse to prep me for an appearance on *Throwdown with Bobby Flay*. The show was victorious for me (and Chef Flay proved to be an extremely gracious loser), so it all turned out great . . . but boy was I disappointed that we never filmed the original show!

In my mind, sugar was going to be the star of at least one of the episodes of the series for the simple reason that its role in baking is so much vaster than you would think. It does way more than simply add sweetness to a dessert. In fact, if the only challenge in baking without sugar were to teach the palate how to adjust to less sweetness, this would be a very short book. In removing sugar from a pastry, you are not just removing its source of sweetness, you are also changing the chemical nature of your baking, which has numerous unexpected consequences.

Once you learn how sugar works in baking, you'll understand better how removing it affects the shelf life, texture, appearance, and, of course, taste in desserts. Here are the myriad roles that sugar plays in baking.

1. Adds sweetness. The best-known attribute sugar brings to the table is sweetness. It makes bitter foods more palatable and makes desserts more tempting. It is often considered addictive—the more you eat, the more you want. What your palate reads as "just right" in terms of sweetness is highly malleable as well. You can train yourself to enjoy less sweetness in your pastries simply by eating more and more desserts made with less sugar. Conversely, your palate will crave highly sweetened foods if you regularly present it with such.

2. Attracts and holds moisture. Sugar is hygroscopic, which means it grabs moisture in the air and absorbs it into your food, making your baked goods moister. It also binds to the water molecules that already exist in your food, thereby slowing moisture loss in that way as well. Both the drawing in of moisture from the air and keeping it within the pastry help prevent staleness and extend shelf life. The desserts in this book do not stay as fresh as those made with loads of sugar, so be sure to share what you've made within a day or two to enjoy them at their best.

3. Aids in browning. Two different reactions work together to make pastries bake to a lovely golden brown: caramelization and the Maillard reaction. Caramelization takes place when the sugars within a food melt and then create a deep brown color and new flavors. The Maillard reaction is the result of heating together certain sugars and proteins, producing new molecules that are brown in color and rich in flavor. Without sugar, baked goods don't have the necessary ingredient to turn golden brown, and these low-sugar pastries tend to be paler in color. When baking, we often go by color to determine doneness, so in these recipes train your eye to recognize a lighter shade of brown as an indicator of when to pull something from the oven.

4. Tenderizes pastries. The addition of sugar in a recipe helps to prevent gluten formation. Gluten is the long, stretchy bands of proteins that form when you mix flour and liquid together. In bread making, gluten is ideal; you get hearty, chewy loaves when your dough has a lot of gluten development. In cakes and cookies, however, gluten is the enemy, leading to tough and dense desserts. Sugar acts like a shield between flour and liquid, preventing gluten strands from developing. The more sugar in your product, the less likely you will end up with something tough. The sweetest of cakes and cookies are often touted for their melt-in-your-mouth, velvety qualities.

5. Makes pastries crispy. Sugar liquefies in the oven when it is in a pastry dough or batter. If there is a lot of sugar, it recrystallizes as water is gradually removed during baking through evaporation, and the result is a lovely crisp texture. At the extreme, sugar by itself turns to caramel, which hardens completely upon cooling. Baking with less sugar means that you never quite get that crispy, crunchy, sugary snap that you expect in a traditional cookie, but if you adjust your

expectations to a softer and cakier mouthfeel, you can still make a great cookie.

6. Lowers the freezing point of frozen desserts. If you put water in the freezer, you get ice. If you put sugar-water syrup in the freezer, you get slush, or if your mixture is super sugary, it might not freeze up at all. Adding sugar to a liquid makes it freeze at a much lower temperature than if you didn't add sugar. What does this mean for bakers? It means that when you make ice cream, it's the sugar in the ice cream that makes it scoopable and creamy, and not icy and hard as a rock. For ice creams and sorbets made with less sugar, one trick is to add alcohol to the base since alcohol acts like sugar to depress the freezing point.

7. Inhibits coagulation of egg proteins in custards. Sugar is pesky! In the same way that it gets in the way of gluten development (see Tenderizes pastries, previous), it also keeps the proteins in eggs from bonding together when they are heated so that you can make smooth, creamy custards. Without sugar, custards can get tough and rubbery a lot quicker, so be careful when cooking or baking low/no-sugar custards and pastry creams.

8. Stabilizes beaten egg foams. When you are whipping up eggs, they get foamy and airy and increase in volume—and then they deflate. If you add sugar, the walls of the bubbles that form when the eggs are beaten strengthen and stiffen; think of sugar like the hair spray of egg foams. You can make meringues (beaten egg whites and sugar), angel food cakes (beaten egg whites, sugar, and flour), meringue buttercreams (beaten eggs, sugar, and butter) all because of this chemical attribute of sugar.

9. Incorporates air into solid fats during the creaming process. The crystals in sugar are sharp and jagged, and when baking, we use that to our advantage to create numerous microscopic air pockets in solid fats such as butter. When you mix butter and sugar together, the sugar works like an army of little gardeners (stay with me here) wielding millions of hoes and digging into the butter and aerating it. This is a hugely important step in many baking recipes. Creaming butter and sugar together, as this action is called, sets up your pastry to be light and airy and fluffy instead of dense.

10. Helps yeast grow by giving it food. Yeasts are one-celled organisms that we use in baking breads and yeasted breakfast pastries to make them fluffy and light. They work by eating the sugars that exist in dough and then expelling gas as the by-product of all of that eating. When they expel gas, it causes the bread dough to rise and become full of air. When you are making bread, you add a little sugar to give the yeasts something to eat. Sugars naturally exist in the combination of flour and water as well, so bread dough made without sugar will still manage to find sugars to eat—they just take a little longer to proof.

And you thought sugar just made things taste sweet!

HOW TO STOCK YOUR KITCHEN

Following is an overview of some basic ingredients, equipment, and baking tips that I use in this book. Some of the stock sweeteners are listed in the "substitutions" section rather than here. This is my baking arsenal—with these items and lessons at hand, you can make practically anything!

INGREDIENTS

These appear in the general order of most common appearance in many baking recipes.

1. All-purpose flour. We always bake with King Arthur unbleached unbromated flour. We try to use ingredients with as few chemicals as possible and we are lucky to have easy access to unbleached all-purpose flour through King Arthur. That said, you can use a bleached all-purpose flour for these recipes with no issues; just make sure it is fresh. Yes, flour can go rancid if left out for long periods of time. I store mine in the refrigerator in an airtight container if I know I won't be baking for a while.

2. Cake flour. In addition to all-purpose flour, we also use cake flour. It has a lower protein content than all-purpose flour, which basically means that it creates a more tender product.

3. Unsalted butter. I *always* bake with unsalted butter. Salted butters have varying amounts of salt in them, leaving the salt level of your pastry up to chance. Start with the blank slate of unsalted butter and then add the salt to accent your dessert as indicated. Unsalted butter is also fresher; without salt as a preservative, unsalted butter has a very short shelf life, which means that when you purchase it in the store, it has only been on the shelves a short while. Salted butter, on the other hand, can sit and sit and sit in the dairy case for months at a time because it is preserved. That doesn't sound so fresh to me! If you are not using your butter within the expiration date, store it in the freezer to extend its shelf life.

4. Sugar. White sugar and brown sugar are the most common sweeteners in a baking kitchen. White sugar is made from either sugar cane or beets and refined until it is pure white and rid of all impurities. Brown sugar is sugar before it has been completely refined; in other words, it still has some molasses clinging to it, the source of its characteristic color and caramel-y flavor. Some sugar manufacturers make brown sugar by mixing in molasses with refined white sugar. White sugar should be stored in a covered container at room temperature. Brown sugar, which is soft with moisture, should be stored in an airtight container at room temperature as well. If your brown sugar turns hard, there are a few ways to soften it: either place an apple wedge or a slice of white bread in the container and leave it overnight (the moisture in the apple or bread will soften the brown sugar), or put it in the microwave topped with a wet paper towel for 20 to 30 seconds on high power until it softens.

5. Eggs. We use large eggs in all of our baking. There's nothing wrong with extra-large or medium or any other size at all. Just like there's nothing wrong with being a size 2 or 8 or 12! But if you are sizing a dress for a mannequin, you need to know exactly what size to make so that your dress fits all standard mannequins. When baking, it is the same: you want to know that the size of the egg you are using is the same size as used to test the recipe. With baking (as you've started to see already in reading about the science of sugar), everything matters, so if you are adding more or less egg (that is, a bigger or smaller egg), then it could throw off the proportions of your recipe.

6. Milk. I always have a jug of whole milk in the refrigerator, not just for our morning tea and cereal but also for baking. You can substitute 2 percent milk with little loss in flavor; however, if you substitute 1 percent or skim milk, you'll be missing the flavor that the fat in whole milk brings to your final product. In other words, use whole milk or 2 percent milk for the best results in baking.

7. Heavy cream. Not quite the same as whipping cream, which is often sold next to heavy cream, the latter has a 36 to 40 percent fat content, making it especially luscious and rich in desserts. I use it for custards and ice creams and also, most important, for making crème fraîche (see Tips, page 24).

8. Baking powder. This chemical leavening powerhouse is actually baking soda plus cream of tartar combined together as one leavener. It reacts to liquid and heat and helps make your pastries rise. Store baking powder in a cool, dark place; it doesn't last forever, so test it before using by putting a big pinch in a cup of hot water to see if it fizzes. If it does, it's good to go, and if not, it's time to buy a new can. Baking powder is not interchangeable with baking soda (following).

9. Baking soda. This white powdery ingredient is a common chemical leavener in baking that works by reacting with an acid. When you mix baking soda with lemon juice, buttermilk, crème fraîche, brown sugar, molasses, chocolate, or any other acidic ingredient, it fizzes up and causes bubbles. You can't necessarily see the bubbles in your cake or cookie batter, but know that they are there, helping your final product turn out light and airy instead of hard like a brick. Store baking soda in a cool, dark spot and test it before using by adding a pinch to vinegar or lemon juice to see if it bubbles up.

10. Kosher salt. Many people don't think about the importance of salt in baking. It does the same thing for sweets as it does for savories—highlights flavors. Especially when baking with vanilla, lemon, and chocolate, salt keeps desserts from tasting flat and makes them stand out. Diamond Crystal is the brand we use in our kitchen. I learned to bake in professional kitchens where my chefs only seasoned with coarse kosher salt, so it was the only salt we had in the kitchen. It has a cleaner flavor than table salt, and its larger crystals make it easier to control the amount of salt you add to your food. Thus in all of my pastry recipes, I use only kosher salt. If you only have table salt, you will want to use just over half the amount of salt listed, since it's a lot finer and thus takes less space in the measuring spoon.

11. Chocolate. If there is one ingredient that I would encourage all bakers to splurge on and buy the very best of, it would be chocolate. We are a nation of chocolate lovers and once you start working with high-quality chocolates for both baking and eating, you'll realize how a lower-quality chocolate is just a shadow of what a great one can be. Unsweetened chocolate is just chocolate liquor (ground cacao beans) without any added sugar or dairy. Bittersweet to semisweet chocolates contain varying amounts of sugar, with the higher the percentage of cacao content listed on the chocolate, the more bitter the chocolate. Unsweetened chocolate is sometimes listed as 99 percent (it contains less than 1 percent vanilla and the emulsifier lecithin), whereas semisweet chocolate ranges around 50 to 60 percent and bittersweet is roughly everything else in between. The percentage refers to the amount of cocoa liquor in the chocolate, leaving the remaining composition of the chocolate to be mostly sugar. And then there's milk and white chocolate. Milk chocolate has even more sugar, less chocolate liquor, and, of course, milk, whereas white chocolate has no chocolate liquor whatsoever (chocolate snobs will remind you that it is technically not chocolate) and instead is composed of cocoa butter, milk, sugar, and flavorings. For this book we focus on using only bittersweet chocolate with a cacao content of 68 percent. The brands I like best are Tcho, Valrhona, Mast Brothers, and Green & Black. You can often find these brands in gourmet grocery stores or specialty chocolate shops, or you can easily purchase them online as well.

12. Nuts. Assorted nuts—peanuts, almonds, cashews, pecans, walnuts, and pistachios—are wonderful additions to many cookies and cakes and other treats. Store these in the refrigerator or freezer since they are full of natural oils, which can go rancid if left out at room temperature for too long. I always toast my nuts for baking and list that in the beginning of the recipes that use them.

13. Yeast. The two most common types of yeast are active dry yeast, which often is sold in little packages in the refrigerated section of the grocery store, and fresh cake yeast, which is sold in little squares next to the butter and cream in the dairy section. Active dry is usually easier for home cooks because it has a long shelf life; fresh cake goes moldy after a few weeks so unless you know you'll be using it soon, it's often easier to buy active dry. Instant active dry yeast is interchangeable for active dry; as its name suggests, it acts faster than regular active dry yeast, and you don't need to add it to warm water before using as you do the regular.

EQUIPMENT

Many of these recipes rely on basic equipment that you likely have in your kitchen already: baking sheets, bowls, spatulas, whisks, knives, parchment paper. Here I list a few things that might not be on your radar—but should be!

1. Basic pans. If you are just outfitting your kitchen, here are the essentials you need to bake the recipes in this book and most any other baking book:

• Standard 12-cup muffin tin

• 9-by-5-in [23-by-13-cm] glass, metal, or ceramic loaf pan

• 9-by-13-in [23-by-33-cm] glass, metal, or ceramic baking or roasting pan

• 8-in [20-cm] or 9-in [23-cm] cake pan with sides at least 2 in [5 cm] high

• A baking sheet that has rimmed sides and measures 13 by 18 in [33 by 46 cm] and/or a rimmed jelly-roll pan that measures 10 by 15 in [25 by 38 cm] or 12 by 17 in [30.5 by 43 cm]

• 9-in [23-cm] ceramic or glass pie plate or a few disposable aluminum pie tins

2. Bench scraper. A rectangular metal tool with either a wooden or plastic handle, these are indispensable for cleaning your work station and for cutting and trimming bread and tart doughs. I sometimes use them as emergency spatulas when I need to lift or transfer something from a baking sheet.

3. Microplane. When I first started baking professionally, the project of zesting of lemons or limes with a chunky box grater or a channel lemon zester was usually doled out as a punishment for not cleaning the mixer properly or coming to work late. It was a laborious task that I dreaded. Since the rise of the Microplane, however, you can't keep me away from the chore of lemon zesting. A long, skinny metal wand with multiple sharp perforations, a Microplane makes quick and easy work of zesting citrus, whole nutmeg, cinnamon sticks, ginger, and, for savory purposes, hard cheeses.

4. Mixer. A stand mixer is a big help in a lot of cookie, cake, and bread recipes. It is a bit of an indulgence, but if you bake with any regularity (or hope to), it opens the door to a lot of recipes that are more easily prepared with the help of its powerful motor. You can, of course, whip egg whites and cream butter and sugar together and knead dough all by hand. It will take a lot longer, but you'll develop some good biceps.

5. Offset spatula. You don't *need* an offset spatula unless you plan on doing a lot of cake decorating, but I list it here because I find that a medium offset spatula can be super-useful for a lot of other things as well. Mine has a wooden handle and a metal blade that is offset from the handle so that if I'm frosting a cake, my knuckles don't get in the way of the cake. I feel incomplete in the kitchen when I'm baking without one nearby. It's really an extension of my hand. I use it to frost things, move things around, clean off my cutting board or

counter, run around the side of a cake or loaf pan or individual muffins to help dislodge them, and even cut and trim things. It's such a handy tool and I have several of them in the kitchen (in case one goes missing!).

6. Piping bag. I like a plastic piping bag that is 18 to 20 in [46 to 50 cm] because it is then large enough to fill with batter or buttercream and still have a large cuff that I can twist to prevent the filling from coming up over the top. We use disposable bags that we rinse and reuse until they spring a leak. Cloth and wax-lined plastic versions are commonly found in stores; be sure to wash these well after each use so they don't smell funky when they dry. If you don't have a piping bag, you can use a heavy-duty, resealable plastic bag with one corner snipped off.

7. Scale. I am so dependent upon my digital kitchen scale that measures in grams and has a tare function (you can zero it out after you have weighed something on it, allowing you to continue to weigh different ingredients into the same bowl) that I can hardly believe when I hear someone does not bake with a scale. That's like saying you still use a typewriter to write letters (and that you still *write* letters!), or you don't brush your teeth with a toothbrush. Invest in a kitchen scale. I promise you won't regret it. Your recipe measurements will always be accurate, and you'll improve your baking significantly with this one easy purchase.

8. Sieve. A fine wire-mesh strainer or sieve is essential when making custards and ice cream for a smooth, silky final product. Get one with tiny holes so it catches all of the bits of overcooked eggs and shell and such.

TIPS

1. How to scrape a vanilla bean. First, make sure your vanilla bean is soft and plump. If it is hard and brittle, it has dried out and you'll want to rehydrate it by soaking it in warm water for a few hours before using. (To prevent beans from drying, store them in an airtight container in a cool, dry, dark place.) Lay the bean on its side and press it flat so it lies on the counter. Using the tip of a paring knife, pierce it at one end and then slide the knife down the length of the bean, splitting it in half until you get to the other end. Spread the bean out so the seeds are exposed and then scrape the seeds from the bean with the back of the knife. Scrape the seeds that collect on the knife into your batter or custard base or whatever. Scrape the vanilla bean again to ensure you get all of the potent seeds. The scraped pod can be thrown into a bin of sugar and in a few days, you'll have vanilla sugar.

2. How to make crème fraîche. You can buy crème fraîche in many supermarkets, but there's really no need. It's really easy to make and is one of my favorite baking ingredients. Simply place 960 g/4 cups of heavy cream into a container, add about 60 g/¼ cup of buttermilk, and stir to blend. Cover and leave the cream mixture at room temperature in a warm area of your kitchen for at least 12 hours. Then, stir the cream with a wooden spoon for 15 to 20 seconds. If it has not thickened, cover again and return to a warm place for another 3 to 4 hours. Check again and keep stirring until it thickens. Once it has thickened, you have successfully made crème fraîche! Store it in the refrigerator until ready to use; it will keep for up to 3 weeks. To make more, you can use the crème fraîche that you have in place of the buttermilk in the basic recipe: take 960 g/4 cups of heavy cream, add about 60 g/¼ cup of crème fraîche, and follow the directions. Once you have crème fraîche in your refrigerator, keep making it so you will always have it. Use it instead of heavy cream in cooking and instead of sour cream in baking and eating.

3. How to calibrate your oven. I've yet to walk into a kitchen, whether home or professional, in which the ovens didn't need some sort of adjustment. Ovens that don't get used much tend to have wonky internal thermometers from lack of use, and ovens that are in frequent use need constant regulation of their thermostats to ensure they are heating to the temperature they are set for. Buy an oven thermometer and place it in the middle of the oven. Give your oven at least 10 minutes to heat up and then check the thermometer. If the temperature on the thermometer does not match that of your dial, your oven needs some TLC. A repair person can fix your oven so it is heating up as it should, or you can do as I do at home and make the adjustment in your head. My home oven runs cold, which means that when I turn it on to 350°F [175°C], it only gets to around 320°F [160°C]. So to compensate, I simply set it to 380°F [195°C] and then it bakes perfectly. (Someday I'll get around to calling that repair person.)

4. How to preheat your oven. You don't really need directions on how to preheat your oven, but you might need a reminder about why it is important. If you put a cake or pie or cookies into a cold or even warmish oven and allow the oven to heat up while the pastry is inside, the batter or dough will melt before it cooks, and the precious air bubbles you've worked hard to incorporate will peter out. Leaden and dense pastries are the awful result! I've listed "preheat your oven to XXX°F [YYY°C]" at the beginning of the recipes for a reason. Do it before you start and then only put items into your oven once it has fully come to temperature. When you hear that pastry takes patience, this is what they mean. Wait those 10 minutes! Your pastries will thank you.

5. How to grate ginger. Grating fresh ginger can be a frustrating task—it gets stringy and you feel like you're grating more of your knuckles than the ginger—until you learn this nifty trick: Place the ginger in the freezer and when it is completely frozen, use the rounded part of a spoon to easily scrape off the peel. Grate to your heart's content. You'll have a heap of grated ginger in no time.

HOW TO SUBSTITUTE FOR SUGAR

To work around not using refined white sugar, I loved exploring baking with these ingredients. Not all of these made their way into the recipes here, but I offer them up as well as possibilities for you to play with in your baking. I made a conscious decision not to include artificial sweeteners. I've never liked the various aftertastes that each one brings, and I wanted to develop recipes that I'd feel comfortable serving anyone looking to reduce refined white sugar consumption.

1. Maple syrup. Maple is the boiled sap from the maple tree. It has a buttery, warm flavor (maybe it just seems buttery and warm to me because I associate it with a big pile of pancakes), and it adds a distinctive flavor to all of the desserts it is used in. We use grade B maple syrup, which means that it comes from tapping maple trees of their sap late in the winter when it is a bit warmer and the sap is more concentrated. It's darker in color than grade A, rich, and caramel-y, and offers the most flavor bang for the buck in baking. Once opened, maple syrup should be stored in the refrigerator where it will last about 6 months. If you see mold on the surface of the syrup, discard the whole jar as it may be contaminated. The standard substitution if you want to substitute maple syrup for sugar is 1 cup syrup for 1 cup sugar and then decrease the liquid in the recipe by 3 tablespoons per 1 cup substitution. This results in a dessert of equal sweetness to the original, but I've learned that you can typically halve the amount of sweetness

in many pastries and they will taste just as good if not better.

2. Honey. Depending on where it is harvested and from what flower, honey comes in all different flavors and kinds. As with many ingredients I use in baking, I tend to choose what tastes good to me in its raw state to determine what I use in my baked goods; with so many locally produced honeys these days, I suggest you pick one that you love eating straight from the jar for your baking. Honey can be stored at room temperature when open. It's a bit higher in calories than sugar and also sweeter, so you can use less in your baking and still satisfy your sweet tooth.

3. Molasses. This thick, dark treacle syrup is the by-product of refining sugarcane or beets for sugar. I stock a mild unsulphured molasses in my pantry that adds a spicy warm note to my baking. It is acidic, which means that it reacts with baking soda; cakes made with molasses will always have baking soda in them to release the bubbles and lighten the batter. Blackstrap molasses is extremely thick, strong, and bittersweet. It is the by-product of the final stages of refining sugar and it has the most minerals and health benefits of all the types of molasses but is also the most pungent. For our purposes, we use a mild molasses that is not blackstrap since its flavor is gentler. These molasses, such as Grandma's brand, still confer significant nutrients, though they are not as nutrition dense as blackstrap.

4. Apple juice and grape juice concentrates. When I was buying "fruit-only spread" for our toast at home in an effort to reduce our personal sugar consumption, I noticed that the ingredients were always fruit and then apple and grape juice concentrates. I really couldn't tell the difference and neither could Christopher; in fact we both preferred these to the full-sugar versions because the flavors of the fruit really came through. With that in mind, I reduced apple juice and grape juice concentrates until they became thick and syrupy and used them to sweeten a host of desserts with great success.

5. Vanilla extract and vanilla beans. My favorite flavor by far, vanilla immediately makes your mouth and nose think "sweet" when it's included in a dessert. Vanilla beans are expensive but worth it; their tiny seeds infuse everything they are mixed into with an unmistakable heady perfume. Store them tightly wrapped in a cool, dark place. We also use a lot of vanilla extract in our baking. It's a less expensive, albeit less potent, way of adding vanilla flavor to a dessert. Make sure to get pure, not artificial, extract and store it in a cool, dark cabinet.

6. Almond extract. Like vanilla extract, a trace of almond extract flavoring in a pastry can prime your taste buds to sweetness. Adding a little bit to certain desserts will give you a sense of sweetness without having to use sugar. It is strong, so use it sparingly. I add it to any dessert that has almonds in it, and I also like it with stone fruit desserts. The pit of a stone fruit—apricots, peaches, cherries, nectarines—has a faintly almond taste if you crack it open, and the flavor of the almond extract goes particularly well with these fruits.

7. Cinnamon and similar spices. When you get a whiff of cinnamon, instantly you can "taste" sweetness in your head. Cinnamon brings a heady, gentle sweetness to baked goods and, when used in moderation, can lead your taste buds to think something is sweeter than it really is. I've been using pinches of ground cinnamon in my home baking and eating for years; Christopher's daily oatmeal has a generous grating of cinnamon stick, and he's never once missed the sugar in his breakfast. In addition to cinnamon, other spices like nutmeg, allspice, mace, cardamom, and ground ginger all read as sweet to your taste buds, so use these liberally in your quest for lower-sugar baked goods. For best flavor, buy cinnamon sticks and whole nutmeg, and use a Microplane to grind to order. You'll get infinitely more of a flavor boost than with preground dried spices.

8. Orange juice and pineapple juice concentrates. These juice concentrates make a good, tangy, bright source of sweetness for sorbets, ice creams, and baked goods such as pound cakes and cookies. They are not quite as versatile as apple and grape juice concentrates, which have less of an acidic component to them, but they are still a valuable sweetener in your no-sugar baking list of ingredients.

9. Dates. Learning to bake with dates was a revelation for me. I've tasted dates wrapped in bacon and almonds at fancy dinner parties, and I've had date nut breads and sticky toffee puddings made with dates. But never did I think of them as such a versatile sweetener in pastries. I use plump, soft Medjool dates in my baking; if you don't have a good source for these, you can substitute another type of date. Because of the size variations in different dates, be sure you measure the amount you use in these recipes by volume or weight. Dates have a skin that gets tough and leathery with age. Before using them I soak them in some hot water and a little baking soda, which softens and dissolves the skin. Store dates in an airtight container at cool room temperature for up to 6 months or in the refrigerator for up to 1 year.

10. Other dried fruits. Raisins, apples, apricots, peaches, prunes, and pears are all accessible dried fruits that offer a concentrated natural sugar source. I chop and add them to batters and cookies to give a hit of sweetness to the final product. Store dried fruits in airtight containers at cool room temperature for up to 6 months or in the refrigerator for up to 1 year.

11. Agave nectar. Agave is a sweetener that comes from the agave plant (the same plant that gives us tequila). In its purest form, when it is derived from the sap of the agave and boiled down to concentrate the sweetness, it is similar to maple syrup. However, what is commercially available to us is not as natural as you might think. The process by which the agave plant is converted to create nectar is similar to that used to create high-fructose corn syrup. So while it is a sugar alternative darling for some, it turns out that most agave nectars contain the same amount of refined fructose as that found in high-fructose corn syrup.

12. Stevia. This South American herb has been used as a sweetener for centuries in many countries. It was recently approved by the U.S. Food and Drug Administration (FDA) as a low-calorie sweetener substitute here in the United States. It has zero calories, its glycemic index is zero, and it is extremely sweet, so you don't need very much to sweeten your coffee or tea. It does not act like sugar in baking, so it is best used to sweeten fruits, cereals, and frozen treats.

13. Coconut and coconut milk. Unsweetened coconut and unsweetened coconut milk both have a natural sweetness that I love for baking and cooking. Unsweetened shredded or grated coconut has a much chewier texture than the fluffy white sweetened stuff you are used to seeing on the grocery shelves. It's not quite as easy to add to cookies if you are expecting that soft chewy texture coconut typically brings to a cookie or cake; however, using a little bit for flavor makes non-sugar desserts subtly sweet. Unsweetened coconut milk is rich and creamy and faintly sweet. Use it in puddings and ice creams and as a substitute for whole milk in baked goods.

14. Bananas. All fruits are sweet but because of their starch-like, non-juicy texture, bananas are especially valuable as a sugar substitute when baking. Super-ripe bananas that have turned black on the outside and are soft and mushy inside are so full of natural sugars that when you freeze them, they don't freeze solid because of all their sugar content. They even lower the freezing point of frozen desserts (see page 18). We use this to our advantage to make a few creamy frozen treats in the Fruit Is Sweet chapter. Store bananas in a cool, dry place and wait until they are mottled with black before you use them to bake. If you can't use them right away, peel them and store in an airtight container in the freezer until you are ready to use.

15. Fresh fruit. Incorporating fresh or quick-frozen fruit to certain batters and doughs lends sweetness to these treats, allowing you to minimize the amount of added sugar. It should go without saying, but you want to only use ripe, sweet fruit when baking to maximize flavor. Fruits that I love to bake with include apples, pears, all berries, and stone fruits like peaches, plums, nectarines, and cherries. Melons and grapes are wonderfully sweet as well and can be made into refreshing sorbets, smoothies, and fruit soups.

16. Coconut sugar or coconut palm sugar. This sugar substitute is derived from the sap of young cut flower buds of the coconut palm tree that will eventually become coconuts. It tastes a little bit like light brown sugar and can be substituted one to one for brown or white sugar in baking. I don't use coconut sugar here as I tried to stick to substitutes that you can find in any standard grocery store, but you can buy it online very easily.

CHAPTER ONE

REDUCING WHITE SUGAR

Cutting out white sugar from your diet cold turkey might be a little too jarring to your system at first. I know it was for me when I first embarked on this exciting journey to learn to bake with less sugar. We ease into it here. These are my favorite desserts and baked goods made with at most half or even one-third the typical amount of sugar. You'll find that your taste buds will gradually adjust, and your palate will learn to prefer pastries that are less sweet—especially if they are made with superb ingredients and showcase the delightful flavors of fruits, spices, nuts, and chocolate.

- 75 g/¾ cup walnuts, coarsely chopped
- 385 g/2¾ cups all-purpose flour
- 2 tsp baking powder
- ½ tsp baking soda
- ½ tsp kosher salt
- ¾ tsp ground cardamom
- 3 Tbsp sugar
- 115 g/½ cup cold unsalted butter, cut into 8 to 10 pieces
- 3 ripe medium Anjou or Bartlett pears, peeled, cored, and chopped into small dice
- 180 g/¾ cup crème fraîche (see page 24)
- 2 Tbsp vanilla extract
- 1 large egg plus 2 egg yolks

PEAR-CARDAMOM-WALNUT SCONES

One whiff of these scones baking and I am transported to the Swedish bakery I frequented one summer when I was an exchange student in Stockholm during high school. The intoxicating scent of cardamom filled the air, and my favorite indulgence was a sugar-dusted cardamom brioche roll filled with raisins and walnuts. Cardamom is pretty potent, so you don't need a lot to make an impact. Here, its warm, aromatic, floral flavors are the perfect foil to juicy sweet pears and toasted walnuts.

1. Place a rack in the center of the oven and preheat to 350°F [175°C]. Line a baking sheet with parchment paper.

2. Put the walnuts on the prepared baking sheet and toast for 8 to 10 minutes, or until lightly toasted. Remove from the baking sheet and set aside to cool.

3. Using a stand mixer fitted with the paddle attachment (or with an electric hand mixer), briefly mix the flour, baking powder, baking soda, salt, cardamom, and 2 Tbsp of the sugar on low speed until combined. Add the butter and beat on low speed for 30 seconds to 1 minute, or until the butter is somewhat broken down but there are still pieces about the size of a grape. (Alternatively, use a pastry cutter or two knives to cut the butter into the dry ingredients; proceed as directed.) Add the pears and walnuts and beat on low speed for just a few seconds until the pears and walnuts are mixed into the dry ingredients. (If mixing by hand, use a wooden spoon to mix the pears and walnuts into the dough.)

4. In a small bowl, whisk together the crème fraîche, vanilla, egg, and one of the egg yolks until thoroughly mixed. With the mixer running on low speed, pour the crème fraîche mixture into the flour-butter mixture and beat for 20 to 30 seconds, or until the dough just comes together. There will probably still be a little loose flour mixture at the bottom of the bowl. (If mixing by hand, use a wooden spoon to mix the wet ingredients into the dry.)

MAKES

12

SCONES

5. Remove the bowl from the mixer. Gather and lift the dough with your hands and turn it over in the bowl so that it starts to pick up the loose flour at the bottom. Turn the dough over several times until all the loose flour is mixed in. The dough will be soft and somewhat sticky.

6. Using a ½-cup [125-ml] measuring cup, scoop out rounds of dough and place them on the cooled, prepared baking sheet. In a small bowl, whisk the remaining egg yolk with a fork and, using a pastry brush, coat the tops of the scones with the yolk. Sprinkle the scones evenly with the remaining 1 Tbsp sugar. (At this point the unbaked scones can be stored in the freezer, tightly wrapped in plastic wrap, for up to 1 week. If baking directly from the freezer, add 5 to 10 minutes to the baking time and proceed as directed.)

7. Bake for 35 to 45 minutes, or until the scones are golden brown on the edges and pale golden brown in the centers. Let the scones cool on the baking sheet on a wire rack for 30 minutes, then serve.

8. The scones are best enjoyed the same day you bake them, but they can be stored at room temperature in an airtight container for up to 2 days. If you keep them for longer than 1 day, refresh them in a 300°F [150°C] oven for 4 to 5 minutes. Or store in the freezer, tightly wrapped in plastic wrap, for up to 1 week; reheat from frozen in a 300°F [150°C] oven for 8 to 10 minutes.

- 245 g/1¾ cups all-purpose flour
- 60 g/1 cup wheat bran (I use Bob's Red Mill brand)
- 1 tsp ground cinnamon
- 2 tsp baking powder
- ½ tsp baking soda
- ½ tsp kosher salt
- 2 large eggs
- 70 g/⅓ cup sugar
- 115 g/½ cup unsalted butter, melted and at room temperature
- 120 g/½ cup whole milk, at room temperature
- 180 g/¾ cup crème fraîche (see page 24), at room temperature
- 1 Tbsp vanilla extract
- 375 g/2½ cups blueberries, fresh or frozen

BLUEBERRY BRAN MUFFINS

We have a "snack tray" at each bakery filled with various pastries that collect throughout the day that are deemed not quite up to snuff to sell. Misshapen cookies, sticky buns that aren't gooey enough, a broken slice of coffee cake, make up the bulk of the tray. I love each and every misfit pastry, but my eyes especially light up when I see a decapitated blueberry muffin. Most people go for the muffin top. Not me! I go for the fruity insides packed with gobs of blueberries. The natural sweetness of the berries together with the buttery batter make for great snacking indeed. I knew that when making a blueberry muffin with less sugar, I could use this "inside" info to my advantage: truly the most scrumptious part of an excellent blueberry muffin is the part full of juicy fruit. What these muffins lack in sugar sweetness they more than make up for in bountiful berry goodness. Bran makes them even more tempting and good for you, so you can feel even better about enjoying these hearty breakfast treats.

1. Place a rack in the center of the oven and preheat to 350°F [175°C]. Butter and flour a standard 12-cup muffin tin, coat with nonstick cooking spray, or line with paper liners.

2. In a large bowl, stir together the flour, wheat bran, cinnamon, baking powder, baking soda, and salt. In a medium bowl, whisk together the eggs, sugar, butter, milk, crème fraîche, and vanilla until well combined. Pour the butter-sugar mixture into the dry ingredients and fold gently, using a rubber spatula, just until the ingredients are combined. Gently fold in the blueberries until the fruit is distributed well. The batter may seem lumpy, but don't try to smooth it out.

Continued

MAKES

12

MUFFINS

3. Using a small ice cream scoop or a spoon, scoop a heaping ⅔ cup [150 ml] batter into each prepared cup of the muffin tin, filling the cups to the brim (almost overflowing) and making sure the cups are evenly filled. You might think you have too much batter, but you can fill these to overflowing and then you will get nice tops on your muffins. If you prefer smaller muffins, spoon about ½ cup [125 ml] batter into each cup and decrease the baking time to 25 to 35 minutes; you will get up to 18 smaller muffins.

4. Bake for 35 to 45 minutes, or until the muffins are entirely golden brown on top and they spring back lightly when you press them in the center. There's a lot of fruit in these muffins, so make sure you bake them enough so the insides of the muffins don't get soggy. Let the muffins cool in the pan on a wire rack for 20 minutes, and then remove them from the pan.

5. The muffins are best enjoyed the same day you bake them, but they can be stored at room temperature in an airtight container for up to 2 days. If you keep them for longer than 1 day, refresh them in a 300°F [150°C] oven for 4 to 5 minutes. Or store in the freezer, tightly wrapped in plastic wrap, for up to 1 week; reheat from frozen in a 300°F [150°C] oven for 8 to 10 minutes. The unbaked muffin batter can be stored in an airtight container in the refrigerator for up to 1 day.

CINNAMON SUGAR MONKEY BREAD

BREAD DOUGH

- 180 g/¾ cup whole milk, at body temperature (when you put your finger in it, it should feel neither cold nor hot)
- ½ tsp active dry yeast or 3 g/ 0.1 oz fresh cake yeast
- 280 g/2 cups unbleached all-purpose flour, plus up to about 35 g/¼ cup more, if needed
- 1 tsp kosher salt
- 3 Tbsp unsalted butter, very soft
- 1 egg yolk

- 115 g/½ cup unsalted butter, melted
- 100 g/½ cup sugar
- 2 tsp ground cinnamon
- 160 g/⅔ cup heavy cream

Certain desserts just don't seem destined for a low-sugar makeover. I didn't even attempt to make angel food cake—which relies on sugar to stabilize the egg whites in the batter—or caramels—where sugar is the main ingredient. One of my pastry chefs Jon and I were tossing around other desserts that would be difficult to make with little sugar when he piped up, "MONKEY BREAD!" We both stopped for a second and looked at each other—and the challenge was on! Monkey bread, according to most theories, gets its name from the little balls of dough that bake all together and then you pluck them one by one to eat them, similar to a monkey who likes to pluck at, well, everything. The bread dough is a simple, rich dough that gets dipped piece by piece into butter and cinnamon sugar. Before baking, you pour a cream-butter-sugar mixture over the whole thing and it bakes into the dough, leaving a light caramel topping on the little breads. It's definitely not as gooey and tooth-achingly sweet as a traditional monkey bread recipe, but it is crazy delicious. After a while Jon and I kept making this under the guise of "more testing," but in reality it was just because we loved eating it so much.

1. To make the dough: Lightly oil a large bowl.

2. Using a stand mixer fitted with the dough hook attachment or in a medium bowl, combine the milk and yeast and let sit for 20 to 30 seconds to allow the yeast to dissolve and activate. Dump the flour and salt onto the milk, and carefully turn the mixer on medium-low speed. (Or use a wooden spoon to mix the flour into the milk, and switch to using your hands to mix the dough when it gets too stiff.) Let the dough mix for about 10 seconds. (To prevent the flour from flying out of the bowl, turn the mixer on and off several times until the flour is mixed into the liquid, and then keep it on low speed.) When the dough is still shaggy looking, add the butter and egg yolk.

Continued

MAKES

ONE

8-IN [20-CM] CAKE

3. With the mixer still on medium-low speed, knead the dough for 2 to 3 minutes, or until it starts to come together into a sticky dough. (If making by hand, continue to knead the dough by hand; it will be very sticky and soft, but keep turning it over onto itself and folding it in half and punching it in the middle to encourage the dough to develop more stretchiness.) The dough will be somewhat soft and tacky and have a bit of a stretchy consistency. If it is much stiffer than this, mix in 2 to 3 Tbsp water; if it is much looser than this, mix in 2 to 3 Tbsp flour.

4. Transfer the dough to the oiled bowl. Cover the bowl loosely with a piece of plastic wrap or a damp lint-free cloth. Place the bowl in a draft-free, warm place (78 to 82°F [25 to 28°C] is ideal; an area near the stove or in the oven with only the pilot light on is good) for about 2 hours. The dough should rise until it is about double in bulk. (This is called proofing the dough.)

5. When the dough has doubled in size, dump it out onto a well-floured work surface and stretch it into a long rectangle about 12 in by 4 in [30 cm by 10 cm]. Using a bench scraper or a knife, divide the dough the long way into four narrow strips, each about 1 in [3 cm] wide. Then divide each dough strip into eight pieces so that you end up with thirty-two little nuggets total.

6. Butter and flour an 8-in [20-cm] round cake pan with sides that are at least 2 in [5 cm] high.

7. Put the melted butter in a small bowl. In a separate small bowl, mix together the sugar and cinnamon. Roll each dough nugget into a little ball and dip into the melted butter, shake off any excess butter, and then roll around in the cinnamon sugar. Place the nuggets in the prepared cake pan, close to each other, but with a little space

in between each nugget, to cover the bottom of the pan. When you fill up the bottom of the pan, continue by stacking them on top of each other. When all of the nuggets have been buttered and sugared, drape a piece of plastic wrap or a damp lint-free cloth over the cake pan and let sit in a draft-free, warm place for another 1 to 1½ hours. When the nuggets have proofed—that is, when they have grown in size and feel soft and puffy—they are ready to bake.

8. Place a rack in the center of the oven and preheat to 350°F [175°C]. In a small bowl, whisk together the remaining butter and cinnamon sugar and then whisk in the cream. Pour this mixture evenly over the top of the nuggets (it will drown the nuggets) and place the cake pan in the oven. Bake for 45 to 55 minutes, or until the tops of the nuggets have turned light golden brown, rotating the pan about halfway once during baking.

9. Remove the monkey bread from the oven and let sit for about 5 minutes. Invert the bread onto a serving plate. If there is a little bit of goo on the bottom of the cake pan, scrape it directly onto the monkey bread with a rubber spatula (or whisk in 2 to 3 Tbsp cream or water to thin it out and pour it over the monkey bread). Serve warm.

10. The monkey bread is best enjoyed the same day you bake it, but it can be stored at room temperature in an airtight container for up to 2 days. If desired, rewarm the bread in a 300°F [150°C] oven for about 10 minutes.

- 75 g/¾ cup walnuts, coarsely chopped
- 175 g/1¼ cups all-purpose flour
- ½ tsp baking soda
- 1 tsp ground cinnamon
- ½ tsp kosher salt
- 3 large eggs
- 75 g/6 Tbsp sugar
- 70 g/⅓ cup vegetable oil
- 3 large or 4 medium super-ripe bananas (really ripe—I mean it! Black and spotty on the outside and soft and sweet on the inside)
- 90 g/6 Tbsp crème fraîche (see page 24)
- 1 Tbsp vanilla extract

BETTER THAN FLOUR
FAMOUS BANANA BREAD

If there is one item that I eat the most of at the bakery it would be our banana bread. I'm completely addicted to the ends of each loaf that the bakers trim off before they slice it up to sell on the pastry counter, and often the morning baker will put the day's ends into a little container for me so that when I make the rounds, they are ready for me to start snacking. Except that it's not quite such a little container. Nicole, my executive pastry chef, once put all of the ends together, one on top of another, and it was almost half a loaf. This was when we just had two locations; I don't want to think about how big the ends all add up together now that there are four Flours.

In creating a low-sugar version, I knew it had to have that same super-banana-y taste and tender texture that I love about the full-sugar version. I fiddled around with the sugar amount, getting it as low as I could so that the texture was still moist, while keeping the taste plenty sweet by making sure to use super super-ripe bananas. I also cooked some of the bananas to ensure that the sugars really broke down and came shining through. This recipe will not work with picturesque sunshine-y yellow bananas—you need the brown spotted mushy ones that are full of natural sugar. You will be rewarded with banana bread that rivals the original with less than one-third the amount of sugar.

1. Place a rack in the center of the oven and preheat to 325°F [165°C]. Butter and flour a 9-by-5-in [23-by-13-cm] loaf pan, or butter and line the bottom and sides with parchment paper.

2. Put the walnuts on a baking sheet and toast for 8 to 10 minutes, or until lightly toasted. Set aside to cool.

3. In a medium bowl, stir together the flour, baking soda, cinnamon, and salt. Set aside.

MAKES

ONE

9-IN [23-CM] LOAF

4. Using a stand mixer fitted with the whisk attachment, beat the eggs and sugar on medium speed for about 5 minutes, or until light and fluffy. (Or whip by hand with an electric hand mixer until light and fluffy, about 8 minutes.)

5. With the mixer on low speed, slowly drizzle in the vegetable oil. Be sure not to pour the oil in all at once; add it slowly so it has time to incorporate into the eggs and doesn't deflate the air you've just beaten into the batter.

6. In a medium microwave-safe bowl, mash all but one of the bananas thoroughly with a fork and microwave on high power for about 60 seconds, or until they are hot. (If you don't have a microwave, cook the bananas in a small saucepan on medium-high heat for 1 to 2 minutes, or until they break down and get soft and mushy.) Using a small whisk, whisk in the crème fraîche and vanilla until thoroughly combined into a purée. Mash up the remaining banana and stir into the banana mixture. Add the banana mixture to the egg mixture and mix on low speed until just combined. Fold in the dry ingredients and nuts by hand with a rubber spatula until thoroughly combined, so there are no more flour streaks in the batter.

7. Pour the batter into the prepared pan. Bake for 50 to 60 minutes, or until the top of the banana bread is pale golden brown and springs back when you poke it in the center. If your finger sinks when you poke the bread, it needs to bake a little longer. Let cool in the pan on a wire rack for at least 30 minutes, then pop the bread out of the pan and slice.

8. Banana bread can be stored, tightly wrapped in plastic wrap, at room temperature for up to 2 days. Or store in the freezer, tightly wrapped in plastic wrap, for up to 2 weeks; thaw overnight at room temperature.

- 175 g/1¼ cups all-purpose flour
- ½ tsp baking powder
- ½ tsp kosher salt
- 390 g/14 oz bittersweet chocolate, at least 68 percent cacao content or higher
- 170 g/¾ cup unsalted butter, cut into 5 or 6 pieces
- 4 large eggs
- 115 g/½ cup mascarpone cheese
- 140 g/⅔ cup sugar

FUDGY MASCARPONE BROWNIES

The chocolate-y, rich, indulgent brownies that we make at Flour are made with 400 g/2 cups of sugar for 16 brownies. That's 2 Tbsp of sugar per brownie: go right now and measure 2 Tbsp of sugar and imagine swallowing all of that in one sitting. It's a lot more than you think. All of that sugar is what makes the brownie decadent and luscious.

I wasn't sure if I could pull off a low-sugar version. How would I create that characteristic dense fudgy-ness of brownies without loads of sugar to introduce moisture and richness? How would the brownies bake enough to hold their shape and not just taste like a mass of goo, but not bake so much that they became dry? It turns out that you don't miss the sweetness of sugar in these brownies if you increase the actual chocolate. In fact, you end up with a treat even more chocolate-y (sounds like a good thing to me). And to help the brownie bake moist without coming across as underdone or gooey, we beat in some rich mascarpone cheese that brings the whole thing together to make these brownies just as splendid as the original.

1. Place a rack in the center of the oven and preheat to 325°F [165°C]. Butter and flour a 9-by-13-in [23-by-33-cm] baking pan.

2. In a medium bowl, sift together the flour, baking powder, and salt and set aside.

3. Bring a saucepan filled partway with water to a very gentle simmer over medium heat. Place the chocolate and butter in a metal or glass bowl. Place the bowl over (not touching) the barely simmering water in the saucepan and heat, stirring occasionally with a wooden spoon or rubber spatula, until the chocolate and butter are completely melted and smooth. Alternatively, microwave the chocolate and butter in a microwave-safe bowl in 30-second intervals, stirring after each interval, until melted and smooth.

MAKES

12

BROWNIES

4. Using a stand mixer fitted with the paddle attachment (or with an electric hand mixer; if using a hand mixer, use a large bowl to accommodate all ingredients), beat the eggs and mascarpone on medium speed until smooth. With the mixer on low speed, slowly add the sugar and beat for about 1 minute, or until the sugar is mixed in. Using a rubber spatula, fold in the chocolate mixture.

5. Using the rubber spatula, gently fold the flour mixture into the egg-chocolate mixture until thoroughly combined. (If the bowl you used for the egg-chocolate mixture is too small for folding, transfer the mixture to a larger bowl and then fold in the flour mixture.) Scrape the batter into the prepared pan and spread in an even layer with the spatula (the batter will be thick).

6. Bake for 20 to 25 minutes (but check every few minutes starting at 15 minutes to make sure the brownies don't over-bake), or until a knife slipped into the center of the pan comes out with a few wet crumbs on it. If the knife comes out with liquid batter on it, the brownies need more time in the oven; if the knife comes out with nothing on it, the brownies are probably a bit over-baked and no longer fudgy, but they will still be delicious. Let cool in the pan on a wire rack for at least 2 hours, or until completely cool. (Because these are so moist, they need time to cool and firm up enough to cut.) Cut into 12 pieces.

7. The brownies can be stored in an airtight container at room temperature for up to 3 days. Or store in the freezer, tightly wrapped in plastic wrap, for up to 2 weeks; thaw at room temperature for 3 to 4 hours.

- 115 g/½ cup unsalted butter, melted
- 50 g/¼ cup sugar
- 1 Tbsp finely grated lemon zest
- 2 tsp vanilla extract
- 1 large egg
- 140 g/1 cup all-purpose flour
- 40 g/¼ cup fine cornmeal
- 1 tsp baking powder
- ½ tsp kosher salt

SUGAR DIPPING MIX
- 2 Tbsp sugar
- 30 g/¼ cup finely chopped, roasted and salted pistachios
- 1 Tbsp finely grated lemon zest

CAMERON'S LEMON-POLENTA-PISTACHIO BUTTONS

Full of bright lemon flavor and crunchy with cornmeal and green pistachios, these button cookies are a wonderful pick-me-up treat. Keep the batter on hand for baking up a quick snack, or bake a bunch and pack them in a pretty cellophane bag for a lovely housewarming gift. My young nephew Cameron and I are always talking about planning more time to bake together (we don't see each other as much as I would like), so I created these with him in mind for our next baking project.

1. Pour the butter into a medium bowl and add the sugar, lemon zest, vanilla, and egg. Stir together with a wooden spoon or rubber spatula.

2. In a large bowl, combine the flour, cornmeal, baking powder, and salt and stir to combine. Add the butter-egg mixture to the dry ingredients and mix until well combined. Refrigerate the dough until firm, about 1 hour or up to overnight. If refrigerating overnight, store in an airtight container.

3. Place a rack in the center of the oven and preheat to 350°F [175°C]. Line a baking sheet with parchment paper.

4. To make the dipping mix: In a small bowl, combine the sugar, pistachios, and lemon zest.

5. Roll the cookie dough into balls the size of a large walnut. Roll the dough balls around in the dipping mix, pressing firmly to allow the sugar mix to adhere to the cookies. (You'll likely end up with a little dipping mix left over.)

Continued

MAKES ABOUT

12

COOKIES

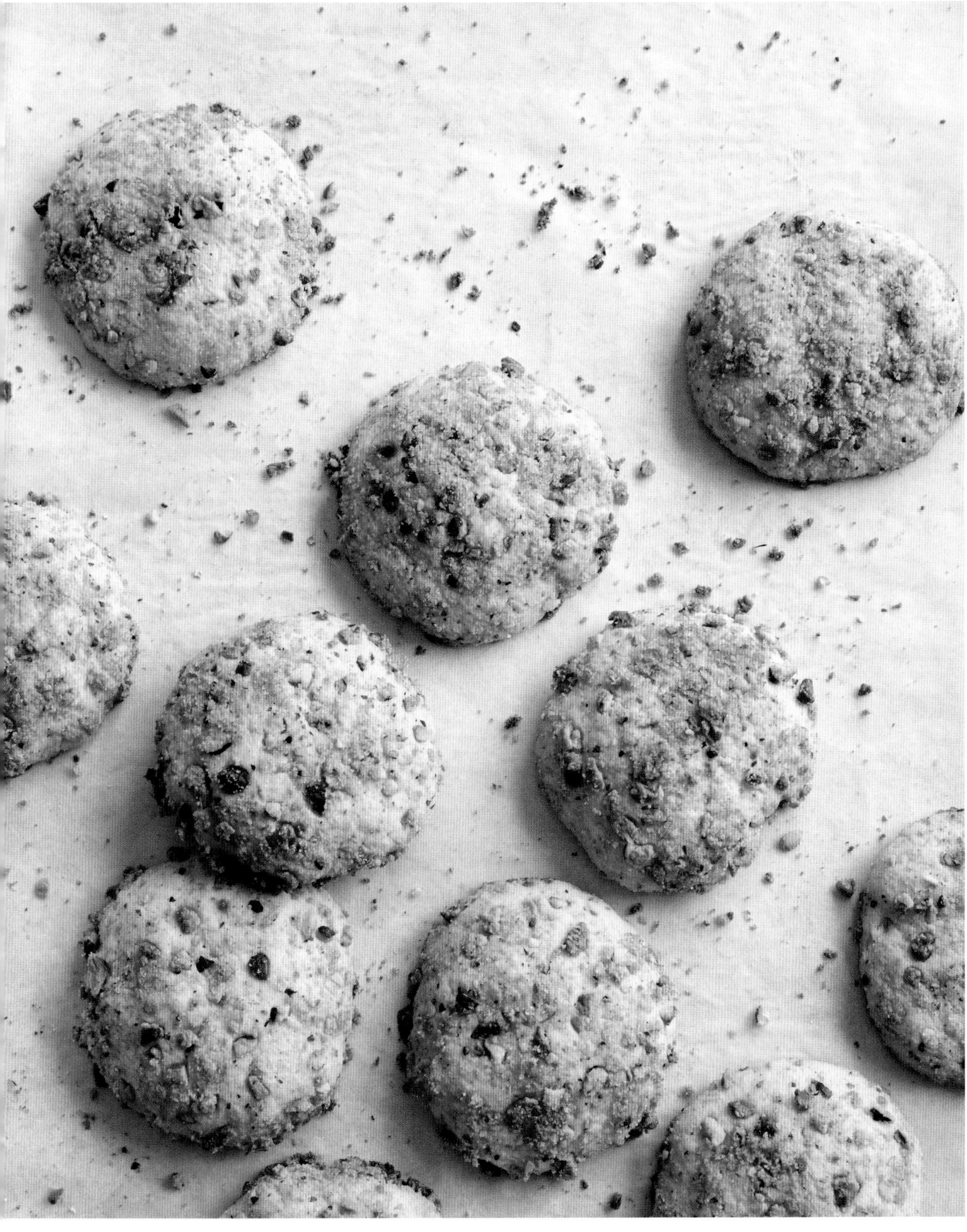

6. Place the cookies on the prepared baking sheet about 2 in [5 cm] apart. Press them flat with the palm of your hand; these don't spread very much on their own. Bake for 15 to 18 minutes, or until they are golden brown on the edges and pale in the center and baked through. Remove the cookies from the oven and let them cool on the sheet for 5 to 10 minutes, then transfer the cookies to a wire rack to cool completely.

7. The cookies can be stored at room temperature in an airtight container for up to 2 days. The unbaked dough can be stored in an airtight container in the refrigerator for up to 1 week or in the freezer for up to 3 weeks (add a few minutes to the baking time if you are baking straight from the freezer); the sugar dipping mix can be stored in an airtight container at room temperature for up to 1 week.

WHITE CHOCOLATE–CHERRY-ALMOND COOKIES

- 120 g/1 cup slivered almonds
- 225 g/1 cup unsalted butter, at room temperature
- 75 g/6 Tbsp sugar
- 2 large eggs plus 3 egg yolks
- 2 Tbsp vanilla extract
- 2 tsp almond extract
- 230 g/1⅔ cups all-purpose flour
- 70 g/⅔ cup almond flour
- 1 tsp baking soda
- 1 tsp kosher salt
- 335 g/12 oz white chocolate, chopped into small chunks
- 200 g/1¼ cups dried cherries, about half of them coarsely chopped

In their full-sugar mode, these cookies are an all-staff favorite, so I knew it would be a challenge to come up with a low-sugar variation that would be equally well received. White chocolate and dried cherries are so sweet already that, by reducing the amount of sugar, you actually don't miss the sugar; in fact, you are actually rewarded with more almond flavor and you can taste the fruit and chocolate much more clearly. They bake brown and crispy on the edges and soft and cakey in the middle, and as one staff member said to me, "These are heavenly!"

1. Place a rack in the center of the oven and preheat to 350°F [175°C].

2. Put the almonds on a baking sheet and toast for 8 to 10 minutes, or until lightly toasted. Set aside to cool.

3. Using a stand mixer fitted with the paddle attachment (or with an electric hand mixer or mixing by hand with a wooden spoon), beat the butter and sugar on medium speed for 5 to 6 minutes (10 minutes if mixing by hand), or until the mixture is well combined, light, and fluffy. Stop the mixer and, using a rubber spatula, scrape the sides and bottom of the bowl and the paddle itself a few times; the sugar and butter love to collect here and stay unmixed. Beat in the eggs, egg yolks, vanilla, and almond extract on medium speed for 2 to 3 minutes, or until thoroughly combined. Again, scrape the bowl and the paddle to make sure the eggs are thoroughly incorporated.

Continued

MAKES

16 TO 20

COOKIES

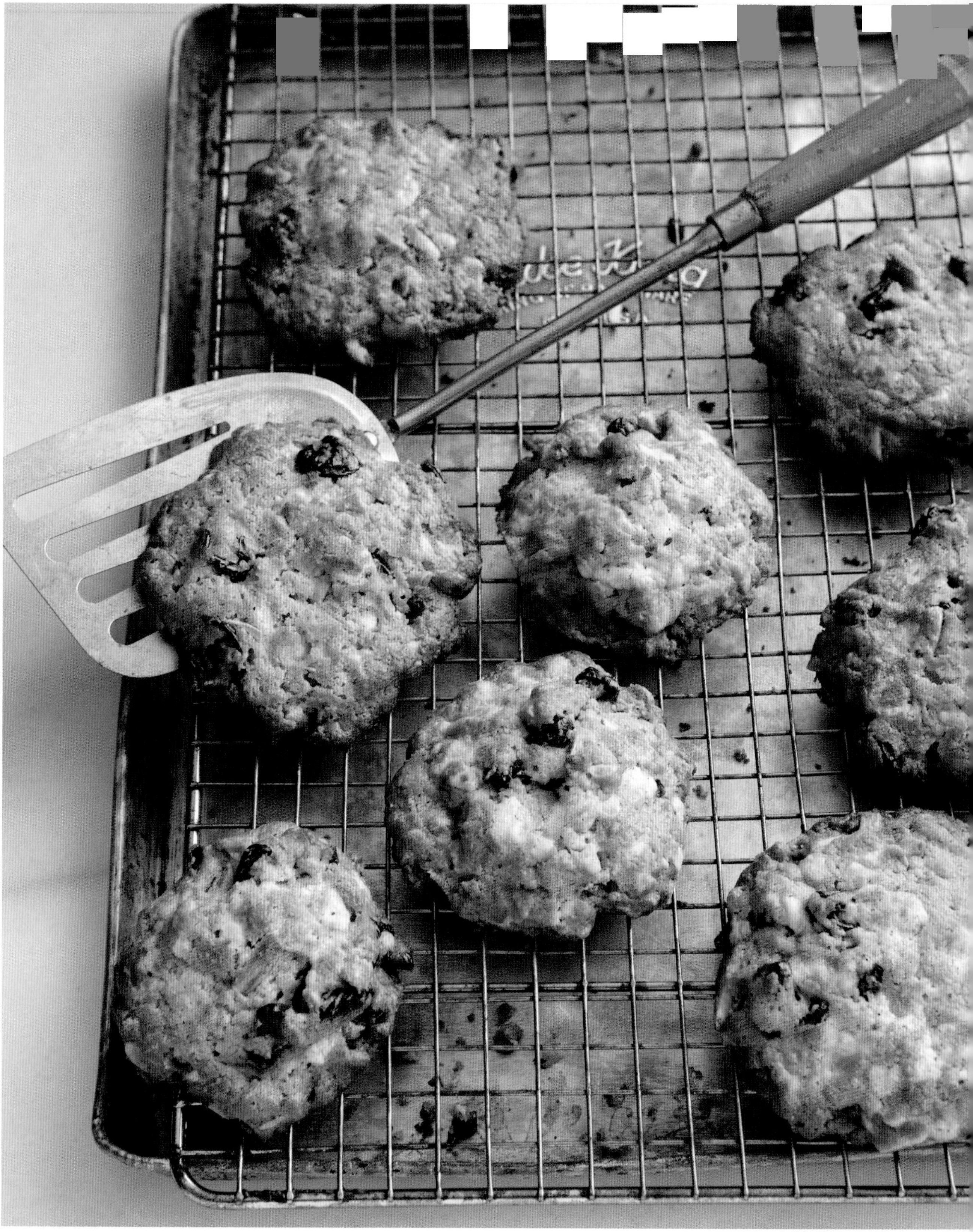

4. In a separate bowl, mix together the all-purpose flour, almond flour, baking soda, and salt. Add the almonds, white chocolate, and dried cherries to the flour mixture and toss to combine. Turn the mixer on low speed (or continue to use a wooden spoon if mixing by hand) and slowly blend the flour mixture into the butter mixture. Mix until the flour is totally incorporated and the dough is completely mixed.

5. For best results, scrape the dough into an airtight container and let it rest in the refrigerator overnight (or at least 3 to 4 hours) before baking. The next day or when ready to bake, place a rack in the center of the oven and preheat to 350°F [175°C]. Line a baking sheet with parchment paper.

6. Using a small ice cream scoop or rounded spoon, drop the dough in balls the size of a ping-pong ball onto the prepared baking sheet about 2 in [5 cm] apart. Press the dough balls down flat with the palm of your hand. Bake for 14 to 18 minutes, or until the cookies are golden brown on the edges and slightly soft in the center. Be careful not to overbake! Remove the cookies from the oven and let them cool on the sheet for 5 to 10 minutes, then transfer the cookies to a wire rack to cool completely.

7. The cookies can be stored in an airtight container at room temperature for up to 2 days. The unbaked dough can be stored in an airtight container in the refrigerator for up to 1 week.

- 75 g/¾ cup walnuts, coarsely chopped
- 225 g/1 cup unsalted butter, melted and cooled
- 75 g/6 Tbsp sugar
- 2 large eggs plus 1 egg yolk
- 2 tsp vanilla extract
- 105 g/¾ cup all-purpose flour
- 150 g/1½ cups old-fashioned rolled oats (not instant or quick cooking)
- 1 tsp baking soda
- 1 tsp kosher salt
- ¼ tsp freshly grated nutmeg
- ½ tsp ground cinnamon
- 120 g/¾ cup raisins, about half of them coarsely chopped
- 120 g/¾ cup dried cranberries

OATMEAL-RAISIN-CRANBERRY COOKIES

This book wouldn't have existed if not for this recipe. When I was playing around with the idea of writing a low-sugar book, I had one and only one priority: the recipes *had* to be so good and so delicious that you could serve them without announcing the caveat that they were made with less sugar. They had to stand on their own as scrumptious and mouthwatering—and it just so happened that they were also low sugar. I started with a classic—oatmeal-raisin cookies—and tweaked and tested until I had a recipe that I could proudly serve at a dessert reception. And that's exactly what we did. These cookies made their debut at a reception welcoming one of my favorite food writers, Mark Bittman, to Boston. He was too busy greeting guests during the reception to actually try the cookies, so I slipped a few in a cocktail napkin and handed them to him as he was leaving. I never followed up with him to see if he actually tried them; but we've stayed in touch since that reception, and I like to think that these irresistible cookies may have had a little something to do with that.

1. Place a rack in the center of the oven and preheat to 350°F [175°C].

2. Put the walnuts on a baking sheet and toast for 8 to 10 minutes, or until lightly toasted. Set aside to cool.

3. Using a stand mixer fitted with the paddle attachment (or with an electric hand mixer or mixing by hand with a wooden spoon), beat the butter and sugar on medium speed for 5 to 6 minutes (10 minutes if mixing by hand), or until the mixture is well combined, light, and fluffy. Stop the mixer and, using a rubber spatula, scrape the sides and bottom of the bowl and the paddle itself a few times; the sugar and butter love to collect here and stay unmixed. Beat in the eggs, egg yolk, and vanilla on medium speed for 1 to 2 minutes, or until thoroughly combined. Again, scrape the bowl and the paddle to make sure the eggs are thoroughly incorporated.

MAKES

16 TO 20

COOKIES

4. In a separate bowl, mix together the flour, oats, baking soda, salt, nutmeg, and cinnamon. Add the raisins (both whole and chopped), cranberries, and walnuts to the flour mixture and toss to combine. Turn the mixer on low speed (or continue to use a wooden spoon if mixing by hand) and slowly blend the flour mixture into the butter mixture. Mix until the flour and raisins are totally incorporated and the dough is completely mixed.

5. For best results, scrape the dough into an airtight container and let it rest in the refrigerator overnight (or at least 3 to 4 hours) before baking. The next day, or when ready to bake, place a rack in the center of the oven and preheat to 350°F [175°C]. Line a baking sheet with parchment paper.

6. With a large scoop or spoon, scoop up balls of dough about the size of a golf ball or ping-pong ball and drop onto the prepared baking sheet about 2 in [5 cm] apart. Press the dough down slightly with the palm of your hand. Bake for 14 to 18 minutes, or until the cookies are golden brown on the edges and slightly soft in the center, rotating the sheet about halfway during baking. Be careful not to overbake! Remove the cookies from the oven and let them cool on the sheet for 5 to 10 minutes, then remove the cookies to a wire rack to cool completely.

7. The cookies can be stored in an airtight container at room temperature for up to 2 days. The unbaked dough can be stored in an airtight container in the refrigerator for up to 1 week.

- Double-Crust Pie Dough (page 55)
- 680 g/4 cups fresh blueberries
- 50 g/4 Tbsp sugar
- 35 g/¼ cup all-purpose flour
- ⅛ tsp kosher salt
- ½ tsp almond extract
- 1 Tbsp freshly squeezed lemon juice
- 2 Tbsp unsalted butter, at room temperature
- 4 ripe nectarines, unpeeled, pitted, and cut into ½-in [1-cm] slices
- 1 egg yolk

BLUEBERRY NECTARINE PIE

I don't eat pie right. I poke off the top and ignore the bottom and dig right into the fruit. I grew up with fruit as my only sweet indulgence and I am a bona fide fruit addict, so when faced with a fruit pie, all I really want is the luscious insides. In this pie, I combine my favorite stone fruit—nectarines—with my favorite berry—blueberry—into a juicy, stain-your-mouth, burst-with-flavor dessert. I use a trick from my first book to pack as many berries as possible into the pie: I cook down half of the berries so they let out their juice and use that to help bind the rest of the berries and the nectarines together. As with pretty much all fruit pastries, your dessert will only be as good as the ripeness and sweet-ness of the fruit you use to make it. So be sure to seek out perfume-y, fragrant nectarines and the plumpest, sweetest blueberries to make this mouthwatering pie.

1. Place a rack in the center of the oven and preheat to 350°F [175°C].

2. Remove the pastry dough from the refrigerator and knead it slightly to make it malleable if it feels stiff. Using a rolling pin, press about two-thirds of the dough to flatten it into a disk about ½ in [1 cm] thick. (Reserve the other one-third for the top.) Generously flour your work surface and the dough disk. Carefully roll out the disk into a circle about 12 in [30 cm] in diameter. Make sure the table you are rolling on is well floured so that the dough does not stick to it; likewise, make sure the disk itself is floured well enough to keep your rolling pin from stick-ing to it. Roll from the center of the disk outward and gently rotate the disk a quarter turn after each roll to ensure that the disk gets stretched out evenly into a nice circle. Don't worry if the dough breaks a bit, especially towards the edges. You can easily patch these tears once you've lined your pie plate.

Continued

MAKES

ONE

9-IN [23-CM] PIE

3. Once the dough circle is about 12 in [30 cm] in diameter, roll it gently around the rolling pin and then unfurl it on top of a 9-in [13-cm] aluminum or glass pie plate. Press the dough gently into the bottom and sides of the plate, leaving a ½-in [1-cm] lip around the edge (to allow for shrinkage in the oven), and using any scraps or odd pieces to patch up any tears or missing bits.

4. Refrigerate the pie shell for at least 30 minutes. (The gluten needs a little time to relax so it doesn't shrink as much in the oven). The unbaked pie shell can be stored, tightly wrapped in plastic wrap, in the refrigerator for up to 3 days or in the freezer for up to 4 weeks. If frozen, the pie shell can be baked directly from the freezer.

5. Blind bake (that is, prebake) the shell so it doesn't get soggy when you eventually fill it with fruit: Line the shell with parchment paper or a large coffee filter and then fill it with pie weights, uncooked beans, uncooked rice, or even well-washed marble-size rocks. Press down slightly on the weights to make sure the shell is entirely filled and place in the oven. Bake for 30 to 35 minutes, or until the shell is brown on the edges and pale and matte when you lift the parchment and peek at the surface of the shell. (If the edges brown too quickly, cover the shell loosely with foil.) When the pie shell is done blind baking, remove it from the oven and let cool on a wire rack.

6. Meanwhile, in a small saucepan, combine about one-fourth of the blueberries with 3 Tbsp of the sugar, the flour, salt, almond extract, lemon juice, and 1 Tbsp of the butter. Cook over medium-low heat, mashing the berries and stirring occasionally, for 3 to 4 minutes, or until the berries, sugar, and flour melt into a gooey mass. Some of the berries will cook into a jam and some will remain somewhat whole. Remove the pan from the heat. Place the remaining blueberries and the nectarines in a large bowl and add the blueberry mixture to it. Stir to combine.

7. Remove the parchment paper and pie weights from the baked shell and pile the fruit into the shell. Dot the fruit all over with the remaining 1 Tbsp butter.

8. On a well-floured surface, roll out the remaining dough into a circle about 10 in [25 cm] in diameter and drape it over the pie with the edge of the circle overhanging the edge ½ in [1 cm] all the way around (you will trim off this excess once the pie is baked). In a small bowl, whisk the egg yolk and brush it evenly over the top crust. Sprinkle the top crust evenly with the remaining 1 Tbsp sugar. Cut four to six slits in the center of the dough to allow steam to escape.

9. Set the pie on a baking sheet to catch any bubbling overflowing fruit juices, and place in the oven. Bake for 1¼ to 1½ hours, or until the top crust is entirely golden brown. If the top of the pie starts to brown too quickly, cover it with aluminum foil during the last 20 minutes of baking to allow the bottom to finish baking without over-baking the top. Remove the pie from the oven and let cool on a wire rack for 3 to 4 hours before serving.

10. Before serving, use a sharp paring knife to carefully trim the edge of the pie, cutting off the excess overhanging dough and leaving a simple, straight edge on the finished crust. The longer you let the pie sit, the more "together" the fruit will be. If you cut into it while warm, the fruit will be especially juicy and the filling, especially runny. The pie can be stored in an airtight container at room temperature for up to 2 days.

DOUBLE-CRUST PIE DOUGH

MAKES ENOUGH FOR ONE 9-IN [23-CM] DOUBLE-CRUST PIE

- 245 g/1¾ cups all-purpose flour
- 1 tsp kosher salt
- 225 g/1 cup cold unsalted butter, cut into about 12 pieces
- 2 egg yolks
- 3 Tbsp cold whole milk

1. Using a stand mixer fitted with the paddle attachment (or an electric hand mixer), beat the flour and salt on low speed for 10 to 15 seconds, or until mixed. Add the butter and beat slowly for 60 to 90 seconds, or just until the flour is no longer bright white, holds together when you clump it, and there are still lumps of butter the size of a pecan throughout. In a small bowl, whisk together the egg yolks and milk and add all at once to the flour-butter mixture. Beat very briefly, still on low speed, about 30 seconds, just until it barely comes together. It will look really shaggy and more like a mess than a dough.

2. Dump the dough out onto a work surface and gather it into a tight mound. Using the heel of your hand, smear the dough, starting at the top of the mound and sliding your palm down the sides of the mound along the work surface, until most of the butter chunks are smeared into the dough and the whole thing comes together. (This technique is called *fraisage* and makes for a very flaky pie dough.) Wrap the dough tightly in plastic wrap and press it down to make a flattened disk. Refrigerate for at least 1 hour before using. The dough can be stored in the refrigerator for up to 4 days (wrapped in another layer of plastic wrap if storing for more than 1 day) or in the freezer for up to 4 weeks.

STREUSEL

- 75 g/¾ cup pecan halves
- 3 Tbsp honey
- 1 tsp ground cinnamon
- ½ tsp ground ginger
- ¼ tsp ground cloves
- ½ tsp kosher salt
- 45 g/6 Tbsp cake flour
- 2 Tbsp unsalted butter, at room temperature

- 300 g/2½ cups cake flour
- 2 tsp baking powder
- ½ tsp baking soda
- 1 tsp kosher salt
- 140 g/⅔ cup sugar
- 225 g/1 cup unsalted butter, cut into 5 or 6 pieces, at room temperature
- 2 large eggs plus 3 egg yolks
- 1 Tbsp finely grated orange zest
- 2 Tbsp vanilla extract
- 240 g/1 cup crème fraîche (see page 24)

MAKES

ONE

10-IN [25-CM] CAKE

VANILLA-PECAN COFFEE CAKE

Sour cream coffee cake has been on our menu since Day One. The method we use to mix this cake is so common within our baking kitchen that many of our cake recipes simply say "mix like SCCC" in the directions. When I opened Flour, the first pastry to get publicly praised by a food writer was this coffee cake. Sheryl Julian, the food editor of the *Boston Globe*, wrote me requesting the recipe and included it in a breakfast pastry roundup she did for the newspaper. (When you are a new business and someone like that praises you, it's like Tiger Woods walking by as you tee off and saying, "Nice shot." You kind of want to tell the world. Which I guess is what I'm doing right now!)

To say I was a bit tentative in trying to make a low-sugar version of this cake is an understatement. Why mess with something that was already pretty much perfect according to hundreds of Flour customers? But on a whim one day, I decided to try it out. I reduced the sugar in the main batter and tweaked the nutty streusel layer and brought the results that evening to the prep crew at my Asian restaurant Myers+Chang. They are used to getting treats from me; I often end my day at the restaurant and will grab a bag of cookies when leaving Flour—and to be honest, they get a touch inured to them. So imagine my surprise when a few minutes after my arrival, the cooks were all abuzz: "Mama, this is so good!" (Yes they call me Mama! Maybe it's all the treats I bring them.) I was floored. Day in and day out bringing them cookies and pastries had elicited no more than a polite "gracias," and with this coffee cake I was suddenly a superstar.

As with most items that contain less sugar, the keeping qualities of this cake are not as good as the regular version—it's best enjoyed within a day of baking. However it's really so good that I doubt you'll have the problem of leftover cake. We never do! Note that you'll need a tube pan with a removable insert for this recipe to easily release this tender-crumbed cake from its pan.

Continued

1. Place a rack in the center of the oven and preheat to 350°F [175°C]. Butter and flour a 10-in [25-cm] tube pan with a removable insert.

2. To make the streusel: Put the pecans on a baking sheet and toast for 8 to 10 minutes, or until lightly toasted. Set aside to cool.

3. In a food processor, combine the pecans, honey, cinnamon, ginger, cloves, salt, cake flour, and butter and pulse for about 20 seconds, or until the mixture comes together roughly and looks like quicksand. Transfer to a medium bowl and set aside; you should have about 1 cup [240 ml]. Alternatively, put all the ingredients in a medium bowl and use a pastry cutter to combine them until well mixed. (The streusel can be stored in an airtight container in the refrigerator for up to 1 week or in the freezer for up to 1 month.)

4. Using a stand mixer fitted with the paddle attachment (or with an electric hand mixer), mix the cake flour, baking powder, baking soda, salt, and sugar on low speed just until well mixed. Add the butter, one piece at a time, and continue to beat on low speed for 3 to 4 minutes, or until the butter is well incorporated into the dry ingredients. The mixture will look like coarse meal. If the butter is a little softer than room temperature, the mixture may come together as a soft dough, which is fine.

5. In a small bowl, whisk together the eggs, egg yolks, orange zest, vanilla, and crème fraîche until thoroughly mixed. With the mixer on low speed, slowly pour about half of the egg mixture into the flour mixture and mix until combined. Increase the speed to medium and beat for about 1½ minutes. The mixture will go from looking thick, clumpy, and yellowish to light, fluffy, and whitish. Stop the mixer once or twice during the mixing and scrape down the sides and bottom of the bowl with a rubber spatula to make sure all the ingredients

are mixed in. Decrease the speed to low, add the remaining egg mixture, and beat for about 30 seconds, or until combined. Again, stop once or twice during the mixing to scrape down the sides and bottom of the bowl.

6. Spoon about 1 cup [240 ml] of the batter into the streusel and fold the streusel and batter together until well mixed. (This step helps keep the streusel from sinking directly to the bottom of the pan during baking.) Scrape all of the non-streusel batter into the prepared pan and smooth the top. Then top with the streusel batter, spreading it in an even layer and smoothing it out.

7. Bake for 40 to 50 minutes, or until the center of the cake springs back when you press it and the top is pale golden brown. Let cool in the pan on a wire rack for at least 3 hours, or until completely cool, then run a paring knife around the edge of the pan and carefully pop out the cake and the removable insert. Run the knife around the bottom of the pan and invert onto a wire rack or plate, gently shaking until the cake pops out; then top with a second wire rack or plate and flip so it is right-side up.

8. The cake can be stored in an airtight container at room temperature for up to 2 days. Or store in the freezer, tightly wrapped in plastic wrap, for up to 2 weeks; thaw overnight at room temperature.

COCONUT CHIFFON CAKE
WITH COCONUT GLAZE

- 200 g/2 cups sifted cake flour (if measuring by volume, sift the flour first and then measure)
- 140 g/⅔ cup granulated sugar
- 1 Tbsp baking powder
- 1 tsp kosher salt
- 80 g/1 cup shredded unsweetened coconut
- 100 g/½ cup vegetable oil, such as canola
- 7 large eggs, separated
- 240 g/1 cup coconut milk
- 1 Tbsp vanilla extract

COCONUT GLAZE

- 70 g/½ cup confectioners' sugar
- 2 Tbsp coconut milk
- 2 Tbsp shredded unsweetened coconut

- Shredded unsweetened coconut for garnish

I adore a light, fluffy coconut cake, and in the first *Flour* cookbook I included one of my favorite recipes: Toasted Coconut Angel Food Cake. Angel food cakes by nature have a lot of sugar in them. They are made with all egg whites, which can make a cake tough (think egg white omelettes, which are often tough and dry), and the antidote to dryness in baking is often sugar. Add sugar to something and it not only makes it sweeter but also much moister.

To make a moist, delicious, and light coconut cake but without as much sugar, I decided to go the chiffon cake route. Chiffon cakes look and taste similar to angel food cakes, but they are made with egg yolks and have added oil mixed into the batter, which makes them rich and tender. I also use full-fat coconut milk; make sure to stir before measuring to combine the coconut cream into the coconut water. I was able to decrease the amount of sugar in this cake to 140 g/⅔ cup (versus 300 g/ 1½ cups in my angel food cake recipe) and still create a remarkably tender cake full of sweet coconut flavor with a barely sweet coconut-y glaze. You'll need a 9-in [23-cm] tube pan with a removable bottom for this recipe.

1. Place a rack in the center of the oven and preheat to 350°F [175°C].

2. In a large bowl, using a rubber spatula or wooden spoon, stir together the cake flour, 70 g/⅓ cup of the granulated sugar, the baking powder, salt, and coconut until combined. In a small bowl, whisk together the vegetable oil, the egg yolks, coconut milk, and vanilla. Set both bowls aside.

Continued

MAKES

ONE
9-IN [23-CM] CAKE

3. Using a stand mixer fitted with the whisk attachment (or with an electric hand mixer), whip the egg whites on medium speed for 1 to 2 minutes, or until they are frothy and the tines of the whisk leave a trail in the whites. Slowly add the remaining 70 g/⅓ cup granulated sugar and continue to whip for 2 to 3 minutes more, or until the whites get a bit glossy and hold a soft peak when you raise the whisk from the whites.

4. Make a well in the center of the dry ingredients and pour in the wet ingredients. Using a rubber spatula, stir the two together to make a batter. When the two are well combined, take a few large spoonfuls of the beaten egg whites and using a rubber spatula, fold into the batter. Add the rest of the whites and fold gently until well combined.

5. With a rubber spatula, scrape the batter into a 9-in [23-cm] ungreased tube pan with a removable bottom. Bake for 35 to 45 minutes, or until the cake is pale golden brown and springs back when you poke it in the center. Remove it from the oven and let cool upside down on a wire rack supported by the inner tube. When the cake is cool, first run a knife around the sides of the pan to slip off the pan, then along the inside of the tube and the bottom to loosen the cake. Quickly invert onto a wire rack or plate and then pop it right-side up onto a wire rack or serving plate.

6. To make the glaze: In a bowl, whisk together the confectioners' sugar, coconut milk, and coconut until well mixed and somewhat thick but still easy to pour.

7. Spoon the glaze over the top and sides of the cake, allowing the extra glaze to drip off the cake. Transfer the cake to a serving plate if it is not already on one. Sprinkle with more coconut, if you like.

8. The glazed cake can be stored in an airtight container at room temperature for up to 2 days.

- 360 g/3 cups cake flour
- 1 tsp baking powder
- ½ tsp baking soda
- ½ tsp kosher salt
- 240 g/1 cup crème fraîche (see page 24)
- 3 Tbsp whole milk
- 4 large eggs plus 1 egg yolk
- 175 g/¾ cup plus 2 Tbsp sugar
- 1 vanilla bean
- 340 g/1½ cups unsalted butter, melted and cooled to room temperature

FLUFFY CHOCOLATE GANACHE FROSTING

- 360 g/1½ cups heavy cream
- 340 g/12 oz chopped bittersweet chocolate or chocolate chips
- 115 g/½ cup unsalted butter, cut into 6 to 8 pieces, at room temperature

YELLOW BIRTHDAY CAKE
WITH FLUFFY CHOCOLATE GANACHE FROSTING

A few years ago, some intrepid passionate professors at Harvard started a basic science class called "Science and Cooking." It was an introductory chemistry class in which they hoped to interest students in learning about chemistry by tapping into their obsession with food. It worked! It quickly became hugely popular, and there's currently a wait list of more than three hundred students wanting to take the class.

The professors reached out to various top chefs around the world to see if they would offer some real-life perspective on how professional chefs use chemistry and science in their everyday work. They went for the gusto, asking food luminaries like Ferran Adrià, David Chang, Dan Barber, and José Andrés, and amazingly, all said yes. As a local pastry chef, I was asked by the professors if I wanted to take on a lecture. I looked at the list of chefs and immediately realized that "which one of these does not look like the other" was at play, and there was no way I could be a part of this.

But they were ever gracious and insisted that I try, and so we embarked upon a class outline that miraculously they approved. I quaked in my shoes giving that first lecture, but as the years have gone on, it's become one of the events I look forward to all year.

Why share with you this long story? The first lecture I ever gave was a simple overview of what happens when you bake a basic yellow cake from a chemistry point of view. I made a yellow cake with no baking powder, another with no baking soda, one with twice the leavening, etc. I also baked one with half the sugar to show how, without the extra sugar, not only was it not as sweet, but it also wasn't as tender—except that it didn't really work out that way. In fact some students actually preferred the half-sugar cake and it made me rethink how much sugar we automatically

MAKES

DOUBLE-LAYER
8-IN [20-CM] CAKE

put into our cakes. The half-sugar cakes were delicious and soft and wonderful.

This cake will not stay quite as fresh as one made with 400 g/2 cups of granulated sugar (as the original recipe calls for) and 200 g/1 cup of confectioners' sugar in the frosting, so it's best enjoyed within a day of baking. It is perfectly sweet even at less than half the sugar.

1. Place a rack in the center of the oven and preheat to 350°F [175°C]. Butter and flour two 8-in [20-cm] round cake pans, or butter the pans and line the bottoms with parchment paper.

2. In a medium bowl, stir together the cake flour, baking powder, baking soda, and salt. In another bowl, whisk together the crème fraîche and milk until combined. Set both bowls aside.

3. Using a stand mixer fitted with the whisk attachment (or with an electric hand mixer), whip the eggs and egg yolk on medium speed for 10 to 15 seconds, or until the eggs are frothy. Add the sugar, increase the speed to medium-high, and beat for 3 to 4 minutes, or until the mixture is thick, light, and lemon colored. Slit the vanilla bean from top to bottom, open it up, and scrape the tiny black seeds into the egg mixture. Whip for 1 minute more to combine the vanilla into the eggs.

4. With the mixer on low speed, slowly drizzle the melted butter into the egg mixture, taking care to pour the butter down the sides of the bowl. (If you pour it into the middle of the bowl, the whisk will spray the butter all around.)

5. Turn off the mixer and add about one-third of the dry mixture to the mixer bowl, turn the mixer to low speed, and mix until the dry ingredients are just barely mixed in. Turn off the mixer, scrape the sides of the bowl with a rubber spatula, add about half of the crème fraîche mixture, and mix again

on low speed until the crème fraîche is just barely mixed in. Repeat with another one-third of the dry, and then the remaining crème fraîche, making sure to scrape the bowl thoroughly after each addition. Finish with the remaining dry mixture, mixing by hand with a rubber spatula until all of the ingredients are thoroughly combined.

6. Scrape the batter into the prepared pans, dividing equally. Bake for 30 to 35 minutes, or until the cakes spring back when you press them in the center with your finger. Let cool completely in the pans on a wire rack.

7. Meanwhile, make the frosting: Heat 240 g/ 1 cup of the cream in a small saucepan over medium-high heat until it just comes under a boil. Place the chocolate in a medium bowl and pour the hot cream on top. Whisk together until thoroughly combined. Let the ganache cool for at least 30 minutes, or until it is warm to the touch and no longer hot. Whisk in the butter, bit by bit, until it is thoroughly mixed in.

8. Using a stand mixer fitted with the whisk attachment and a clean bowl (or with an electric hand mixer or by hand with a whisk), whip the remaining 120 g/1/2 cup cream until it holds soft peaks that droop a little when the whisk is lifted. When the chocolate mixture is completely cool to the touch, fold in the whipped cream. Set aside.

Continued

9. When the cakes are completely, totally cool (if they are at all warm, the frosting will melt off and it will be a mess), remove them from the pans. Using a long serrated knife, trim the tops of the cakes so they are level (they will have rounded a bit in the oven; these top scraps make for great nibbling). Place one cake on a plate or cake pedestal and spoon a scant 1 cup [240 ml] frosting on top; using an offset spatula, spread the frosting evenly all the way to the edges of the cake.

10. Carefully place the second cake on top of the first cake (place it upside down so the even, sharp edges will be on the top of your finished cake), and spoon a scant 1 cup [240 ml] frosting on top. Spread the frosting thinly to the edges and down the sides of the cake, smoothing it as well as you can and covering the entire cake with a thin layer of frosting. This layer of frosting is called a crumb coat; it keeps loose crumbs from migrating to the surface of the finished cake. At this point, refrigerate the cake for about 30 minutes to help set the crumb coat and the frosting between the layers. Chill the remaining frosting as well to firm it up a bit.

11. Remove the frosting and cake from the refrigerator, and rewhip the frosting with a whisk to fluff it up. Spoon about 1 cup [240 ml] frosting on the cake and spread it evenly across the top and sides again. This is the final finishing layer of frosting. Fill a piping bag fitted with a star or small round tip with the remaining frosting, and pipe an edge along the top or the bottom edge of the cake or both, as desired.

12. The frosted cake can be stored in an airtight container at room temperature for up to 1 day.

CHAPTER TWO

JUST CHOCOLATE

Bittersweet chocolate contains anywhere from 5 to 15 grams of sugar per 1 ounce of chocolate, hardly rendering it sugar-free. However, if you use a truly bittersweet chocolate, you'll minimize the total sugar content in these recipes and, except for the sugar in the chocolate, each one of them is completely sugarless. In some instances you'll not notice the difference; truffles and mousses have enough chocolate in them that they are plenty rich and delicious on their own. Some of them skirt the line of super-bittersweet, which honestly are my favorite recipes. The deeply flavorful cacao taste in chocolate desserts that have very little sugar is what speaks to me. You can calculate the amount of sugar in the chocolate you use by looking at the nutritional label—it will list grams of sugar per ounce. These recipes all list the ounces of chocolate needed, so you can then calculate how many grams are used in total. In these recipes I used a 68-percent chocolate, which has about 11 grams of sugar per 1 ounce. Based on that, I include how much sugar is in each recipe in total and also per serving.

TRUFFLE FILLING

- 225 g/8 oz bittersweet chocolate, finely chopped
- 240 g/1 cup heavy cream
- 1 Tbsp finely grated orange zest
- 2 Tbsp unsalted butter, at room temperature
- ¼ tsp kosher salt

FINISHING THE TRUFFLES

- About 140 g/5 oz bittersweet chocolate, finely chopped (optional)
- About 120 g/1 cup cocoa powder

CHOCOLATE-ORANGE TRUFFLES

Fine chocolate truffles that you find in an upscale chocolate or pastry store are delicacies that some people spend their whole lives trying to perfect. The creaminess of the filling, the thin, hard chocolate shell, the beauty of the finish—all of these are hallmarks of a well-made confection. But if you are a home cook wanting to make an indulgent and impressive candy, you can make truffles, too! They may not have quite the little touches that the store-bought ones have, but they will be greeted with so much more enthusiasm than those because they are made by YOU! Of that I am sure.

Truffles are simply tiny balls of ganache—that magic recipe of heavy cream and chocolate mixed together until smooth—that are coated in pure chocolate and then either pressed with a design (if you are a fancy chocolatier) or rolled in cocoa powder (the original way and much easier). Truffles actually get their name from their resemblance to the fungus truffle, which looks like a little piece of mud rolled around in dirt. You can finish these in two ways: The easiest is to simply roll them in cocoa powder and then they are done. Or you can dip them in chocolate before rolling in cocoa to give them a little bit more of a finished look and taste. I don't have you temper the chocolate if you go this route (tempering the chocolate makes it harden into a thin, snappy coating, but can be tricky to do), but you will still end up with a wonderful treat. If you are making truffles that aren't coated with chocolate, this recipe has about 88 grams (just under ½ cup) of sugar in total or around 4 grams per truffle. Coating each truffle in chocolate adds an additional 2 grams of sugar per truffle.

MAKES

20 TO 24

TRUFFLES

1. To make the filling: Put the chocolate in a medium bowl and set aside. Heat the cream and orange zest in a small saucepan over medium heat until the cream is scalded—that is, there are small bubbles on the surface of the cream, and it almost, but not quite, comes to a boil. Turn off the heat and let the cream sit for at least 1 hour or up to 3 hours. After the cream has infused with the orange, reheat the cream over medium-high heat until it is piping hot again.

2. Rest a fine-mesh strainer on the bowl of chocolate. Pour the cream through the strainer over the chocolate. Using a rubber spatula or a wooden spoon (not a whisk, which will introduce bubbles into your chocolate and make for a less-smooth truffle), slowly stir the chocolate and cream together using small circles in the middle of the bowl. You'll want to stir all around the bowl to try and get everything to mix together; resist that urge and just stay zen and the chocolate and cream will slowly start to come together. The more you stir, the more the chocolate will blend into the cream until finally all of the chocolate and cream will be one smooth mixture. When you take the time to stir the cream gently into the chocolate, you'll get a smoother, silkier final product.

3. Once the chocolate and cream are well blended, stir in the butter and salt, again taking your time to stir-stir-stir until the butter is blended in. This is the base for the truffles, called ganache.

4. Refrigerate the ganache in a covered container overnight until it firms up. The next day, with a small spoon, scoop out rounded 1-Tbsp-size balls of ganache and roll them around in your hands until they are round balls. Place on a platter and refrigerate for about 10 minutes.

5. Meanwhile, to finish the truffles: If you want to coat your truffles in melted chocolate before you roll them around in cocoa, bring a saucepan filled partway with water to a very gentle simmer over medium-high heat. Place the bittersweet chocolate in a medium metal or glass bowl. Place the bowl over (not touching) the barely simmering water in the saucepan and heat, stirring occasionally with a wooden spoon or rubber spatula, until the chocolate is completely melted and smooth. Alternatively, microwave the chocolate in a microwave-safe bowl in 30-second intervals, stirring after each interval, until melted and smooth. Remove the truffles from the refrigerator and, one by one, dip them carefully in the chocolate by resting the truffle on the tines of a fork, lowering it into the chocolate, and using the fork to gently roll them around to fully coat. With the fork, lift up and remove the truffle from the melted chocolate and place back on the platter. Continue with all of the truffles until they are coated with a thin coating of chocolate. Place the cocoa powder in a bowl. When the chocolate on the truffles is no longer shiny (it takes about 30 seconds for the chocolate to start setting) and is matte, carefully pick up each truffle one by one with a fork, place in the cocoa powder, and roll it around until coated. Remove the truffle from the cocoa powder and place back on the platter. Let the chocolate and cocoa firm up and serve.

6. Alternatively, you can skip the outer chocolate layer and simply place the truffles as they are directly in the cocoa powder and roll them around until coated. This variation is by far simpler and neater, and the results are still impressive and delicious.

7. The truffles can be stored in an airtight container at cool room temperature for up to 3 days.

- 140 g/5 oz bittersweet chocolate, finely chopped
- 720 g/3 cups heavy cream
- 3 Tbsp unsalted butter, cut into pieces, at room temperature
- ¾ tsp kosher salt
- 1 tsp vanilla extract
- Approximately 3-in [8-cm] slab of bittersweet chocolate, at warm room temperature, for garnish

SIMPLE CHOCOLATE MOUSSE

My first baking job was as a pastry cook for Rick Katz at Bentonwood Bakery in Newton Center (a suburb of Boston), who trained me on all of the basics of pastry in the year that I spent with him. He was a patient, strict teacher who drilled into me that the most important way I could improve as a pastry cook was to taste, taste, taste all the time. He didn't just mean to try as many desserts as possible every opportunity I could (although I did do that); he meant that as you are following a recipe, taste every part you can so you know what it is you are making. From him I learned the invaluable lesson of using the best chocolate, the freshest cream, the ripest fruit, and ground-to-order spices.

In this brilliantly simple and eggless mousse that Rick taught me, it's the chocolate that shines. Choose a chocolate that you cannot stop eating when you eat it straight and you will be rewarded with a creamy, deep-chocolate mousse made without any additional sugar whatsoever. Essentially a whipped cream flavored and sweetened with chocolate, the mousse has a touch of butter for richness, and salt and vanilla to highlight the fruitiness of the chocolate. This whole recipe contains about 55 grams (just over ¼ cup) sugar in the chocolate, which is about a tablespoon of sugar per serving.

MAKES

4 TO 6

SERVINGS

1. Put the chopped chocolate in a medium bowl. Heat the cream in a small saucepan over medium heat until it is scalded—that is, small bubbles form on the edges of the cream and it almost, but not quite, comes to a boil. Pour the cream over the chocolate and let it sit for about 30 seconds. Using a whisk, slowly whisk the cream into the chocolate until the chocolate is completely melted. Whisk in the butter bit by bit. Add the salt and vanilla and whisk until combined. Strain the mixture through a fine-mesh strainer and refrigerate in a covered container overnight. Unwhipped mousse can be stored in an airtight container in the refrigerator for up to 5 days.

2. Just before serving, whip up the mousse either by hand with a whisk, with a stand mixer fitted with the whisk attachment on medium speed, or with an electric hand mixer until the mousse is creamy and holds a soft peak, 3 to 5 minutes. Don't overbeat or it will get grainy.

3. To serve, scoop the mousse into bowls. Using the back of a paring knife or a vegetable peeler, scrape the chocolate block to make chocolate shavings and scatter the shavings evenly on top of each serving.

- 140 g/1 cup all-purpose flour
- 1 tsp baking powder
- ½ tsp baking soda
- ½ tsp kosher salt
- 280 g/10 oz bittersweet chocolate, finely chopped
- 85 g/6 Tbsp unsalted butter
- 120 g/½ cup crème fraîche (see page 24)
- 2 large eggs plus 2 egg yolks
- 2 tsp vanilla extract

CHOCOLATE FILLING

- 170 g/6 oz bittersweet chocolate, finely chopped
- 180 g/¾ cup heavy cream

MAKES ABOUT

10

PIES

DOUBLE CHOCOLATE WHOOPIE PIES

These are not for the (chocolate) faint of heart. Dark chocolate soft cookies are sandwiched with chocolate ganache, so you get a double chocolate whammy. One of my testers who is also a baker at Flour loved these so much that he turned them into homemade Devil Dogs with a whipped cream filling. For that variation, roll the cookie dough into oblong tube shapes, bake, and fill with lightly whipped cream when completely cooled. The sugar in the chocolate totals about 170 grams or just under 1 cup, which is about 17 grams per whoopie pie.

1. Place a rack in the center of the oven and preheat to 325°F [165°C]. Line a baking sheet with parchment paper.

2. In a small bowl, stir together the flour, baking powder, baking soda, and salt. Set aside.

3. Bring a saucepan filled partway with water to a very gentle simmer over medium heat. Place the chocolate and butter in a metal or glass bowl. Place the bowl over (not touching) the barely simmering water in the saucepan and heat, stirring occasionally with a wooden spoon or rubber spatula, until the chocolate and butter are completely melted and smooth. Alternatively, microwave the chocolate and butter in a microwave-safe bowl in 30-second intervals, stirring after each interval, until melted and smooth. Whisk in the crème fraîche until thoroughly combined. Whisk in the eggs, egg yolks, and vanilla.

Continued

4. Add the dry ingredients to the chocolate mixture and, using a wooden spoon or rubber spatula, mix until well combined. Let the batter sit at room temperature for about 30 minutes, or until it firms up a bit. Using a small ice cream scoop or a rounded tablespoon, scoop balls that are about the size of golf balls, and place them on the prepared baking sheet 2 in [5 cm] apart to allow for a little spreading. Bake for 12 to 15 minutes, or until the cookies are just barely firm when touched in the center with your finger. Let the cookies cool completely on the baking sheet on a wire rack.

5. To make the filling: Place the chocolate in a medium bowl. Heat the cream in a small saucepan over medium heat until it is scalded—that is, small bubbles form on the edges of the cream and it almost, but not quite, comes to a boil. Pour the cream over the chocolate and let it sit for 20 to 30 seconds. Using a whisk, slowly whisk the chocolate and cream together until the chocolate is completely melted and the mixture is smooth. Let the ganache sit at room temperature for at least 3 to 4 hours, or until it cools and thickens to a spreadable consistency.

6. The whoopie pie filling can be made in advance and stored in an airtight container in the refrigerator for up to 5 days; bring to room temperature for a few hours before using. If the filling is too soft, it will run down the sides of the pies, so make sure it's firmed up enough to scoop before assembling pies.

7. When ready to assemble, spoon a small scoop of ganache about the size of a walnut on the flat sides of half of the cookies. Top with the remaining cookies, flat-side down, pressing together to make sure they stick, and serve.

8. Cookies can be stored in an airtight container at room temperature for up to 3 days.

BITTERSWEET CHOCOLATE POTS DE CRÈME

- 960 g/4 cups whole milk
- 280 g/10 oz bittersweet chocolate, finely chopped
- 2 large eggs plus 4 egg yolks
- 1½ tsp kosher salt
- 1 Tbsp vanilla extract
- Unsweetened heavy cream, whipped to soft peaks, for garnish
- Shaved chocolate for garnish

I adore bittersweet chocolate. I love how it hits you deep and sharp on your tongue with little relief from the sweetness of sugar and how it lingers faintly smoky in your mouth. If you are a milk-chocolate or even semisweet-chocolate fan only, then this custard is not for you. It is rich and powerful and not for those who shy away from strong, assertive flavors. Be sure to select a fabulous eating chocolate as this recipe essentially turns the chocolate into a creamy, silky-smooth custard. Serve it to true chocolate aficionados or people who enjoy examining the various subtleties in coffee or wine—or both!—as you'll be able to taste all of the different flavors within the chocolate here. The salt is essential in this recipe; it keeps the custards from tasting flat and brings out all of the dark chocolate flavors. As with all of the recipes in this book, use kosher salt or half the amount of regular table salt, which is a lot finer. You'll need eight 6-oz [180-ml] ramekins along with a fine-mesh strainer for this recipe. With about 110 grams of sugar (just over ½ cup) in the chocolate in the whole recipe, each custard has just under 14 grams of sugar per serving.

1. Place a rack in the center of the oven and preheat to 325°F [165°C].

2. Heat the milk in a medium saucepan over medium heat until scalded—that is, small bubbles form on the edges of the milk and it almost, but not quite, comes to a boil. Turn off the heat.

Continued

MAKES

8

CUSTARDS

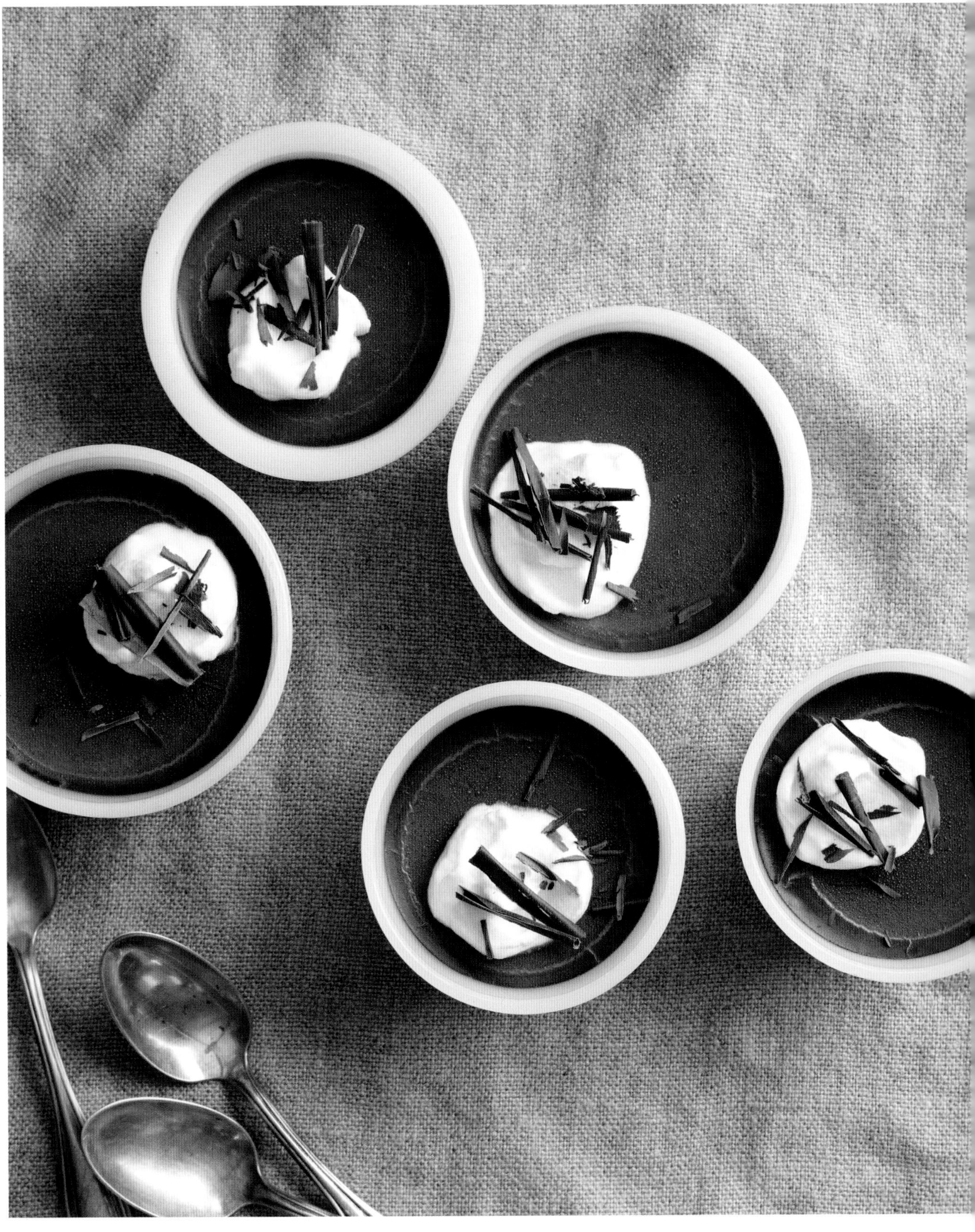

3. Meanwhile, bring a saucepan filled partway with water to a very gentle simmer over medium heat. Place the chocolate in a metal or glass bowl. Place the bowl over (not touching) the barely simmering water in the saucepan and heat, stirring occasionally with a wooden spoon or rubber spatula, until the chocolate is completely melted and smooth. Alternatively, microwave the chocolate in a microwave-safe bowl in 30-second intervals, stirring after each interval, until melted and smooth.

4. Set a fine-mesh strainer over a pitcher or measuring cup. Pour the scalded milk over the melted chocolate and whisk to combine well. Let sit for 2 to 3 minutes and whisk well again to ensure that the chocolate and milk are completely blended. In a large bowl, whisk together the eggs and egg yolks and slowly whisk the hot milk-chocolate mixture into the eggs. Strain the mixture through the fine-mesh strainer into the pitcher. Stir in the salt and vanilla.

5. Arrange eight 6-oz [180-ml] ramekins in a roasting pan with deep sides. Pour the custard mixture evenly into the ramekins. Carefully move the roasting pan to the oven. Fill the pan with hot water halfway up the sides of the ramekins. (This is a water bath and will protect the pots de crème from over-baking.) Cover the pan loosely with aluminum foil. Bake for 35 to 45 minutes, or until just set. Be sure to start checking early; baking time will depend on the thickness and depth of your ramekins and roasting pan. The pots de crème will wiggle stiffly like firm Jell-O when they are done. Carefully remove the roasting pan from the oven and let the ramekins cool in the water bath. Remove the cooled ramekins from the roasting pan, cover with plastic wrap, and refrigerate for at least 4 hours or up to 2 days.

6. Serve the pots de crème, completely chilled, in their ramekins with a little dollop of whipped cream and a sprinkle of chocolate shavings.

- 720 g/3 cups whole milk
- 240 g/1 cup heavy cream
- 120 g/½ cup brewed coffee
- 1 Tbsp vanilla extract
- 280 g/10 oz bittersweet chocolate, finely chopped
- 8 egg yolks
- 55 g/4 Tbsp cream cheese, at room temperature
- 1 tsp kosher salt
- 90 g/6 Tbsp bourbon or other dark alcohol like rum or whiskey

CHOCOLATE FUDGE–BOURBON ICE CREAM

This ice cream is so deep and dark and rich it's almost like eating frozen fudge. The bourbon, chocolate, and coffee all come through and complement each other marvelously. Yum! The better quality of chocolate you use, the more decadent the ice cream will be. I didn't originally intend for this to have alcohol in it, but since this ice cream has no sugar, it freezes way too hard without it. (Sugar lowers the freezing point of ice cream, which means its addition helps keeps ice cream softer and creamier for better scooping.) Alcohol acts like sugar in that it makes ice cream soft when frozen so it doesn't end up a solid brick of chocolate. The addition of cream cheese is a trick I learned from *Jeni's Splendid Ice Creams at Home* cookbook; it helps bind all of the ingredients together and add body to the ice cream. The total amount of sugar in this recipe is about 110 grams.

1. Rest a fine-mesh strainer over a large container and set aside.

2. Combine the milk and cream in a medium saucepan and heat over medium heat until it is scalded—that is, small bubbles form on the edges of the mixture and it almost, but not quite, comes to a boil. Turn off the heat and add the coffee and vanilla.

3. Bring a saucepan filled partway with water to a very gentle simmer over medium-high heat. Place the chocolate in a medium metal or glass bowl. Place the bowl over (not touching) the barely simmering water in the saucepan and heat, stirring occasionally with a wooden spoon or rubber spatula, until the chocolate is completely melted and smooth. Alternatively, microwave the chocolate in 30-second intervals, stirring after each interval, until melted and smooth.

MAKES ABOUT

1½

QUARTS [1.4 L]

4. Pour the hot milk-cream mixture over the chocolate and whisk until well combined. In a medium bowl, whisk together the egg yolks. Slowly ladle a little of the hot liquid into the egg-yolk mixture and whisk to combine. Continue slowly adding hot cream to the yolks, whisking continuously, until all of the cream is mixed in. (This step is called tempering, which allows you to introduce the hot liquid to the cold egg yolks slowly and gently so that you can combine them without scrambling the yolks.)

5. Return the whole mixture to the saucepan and cook over medium heat, stirring constantly with a wooden spoon, for 6 to 8 minutes, or until the mixture thickens and coats the back of the spoon. The mixture will seem thin at first, then it will start to steam, and then it will start to develop a little body and get thicker. Remove from the heat and immediately whisk in the cream cheese until it melts into the mixture. Strain through the fine-mesh strainer into the container. Whisk in the salt.

6. Place the ice cream base, covered, in the refrigerator overnight until completely cold, at least 4 hours or up to overnight. Before churning, whisk in the bourbon. Churn in an ice cream maker according to the manufacturer's directions. When the ice cream has finished churning, transfer it to a storage container and freeze for at least 2 hours to allow it to ripen. During the ripening process, the ice cream becomes harder and smoother and the flavors develop. Due to the lack of sugar in the ice cream, you may need to remove the ice cream from the freezer for 10 to 15 minutes before scooping and serving.

7. Store the ice cream in an airtight container in the freezer for up to 3 weeks.

MINT CHOCOLATE "ICE CREAM"

- 480 g/2 cups heavy cream
- 20 g/½ cup packed fresh spearmint or peppermint leaves, coarsely chopped, or 1 tsp peppermint extract
- 85 g/3 oz bittersweet chocolate, finely chopped
- ¼ tsp kosher salt

CAKE

- 225 g/8 oz bittersweet chocolate, chopped
- 5 large eggs, separated
- 60 g/¼ cup strong brewed coffee, at room temperature
- ¼ tsp kosher salt
- 35 g/¼ cup all-purpose flour

MAKES

8

SANDWICHES

MINT CHOCOLATE ICE CREAM SANDWICHES

After all this time, I've learned a little self-control when I'm in the pastry kitchen. I know now that I don't *have* to eat that chocolate chip cookie batter, or that it's not *essential* that I taste that warm, gooey sticky bun, or that I *can* walk past that tub of carrot cake trimmings. However, when the bakers are trimming a triple chocolate mousse cake, I know my limits. I've never walked by without snagging a frozen end piece of cake and mousse. We make these cakes in large sheet trays and then freeze them until they are firm so we can neatly slice through them. Each time I eat an edge, I think to myself, this is like the best ice cream sandwich I've ever had. So I took the idea of making a thin chocolate cake and filling it with a whipped chocolate mousse that ends up freezing into something quite like ice cream. Infuse the cream with fresh mint and you've got a spectacular summer treat. (Or you can use peppermint extract if you can't get your hands on fresh mint.) The chocolate in this recipe has about 130 grams of sugar in it, making each sandwich clock in at around 16 grams of sugar.

Continued

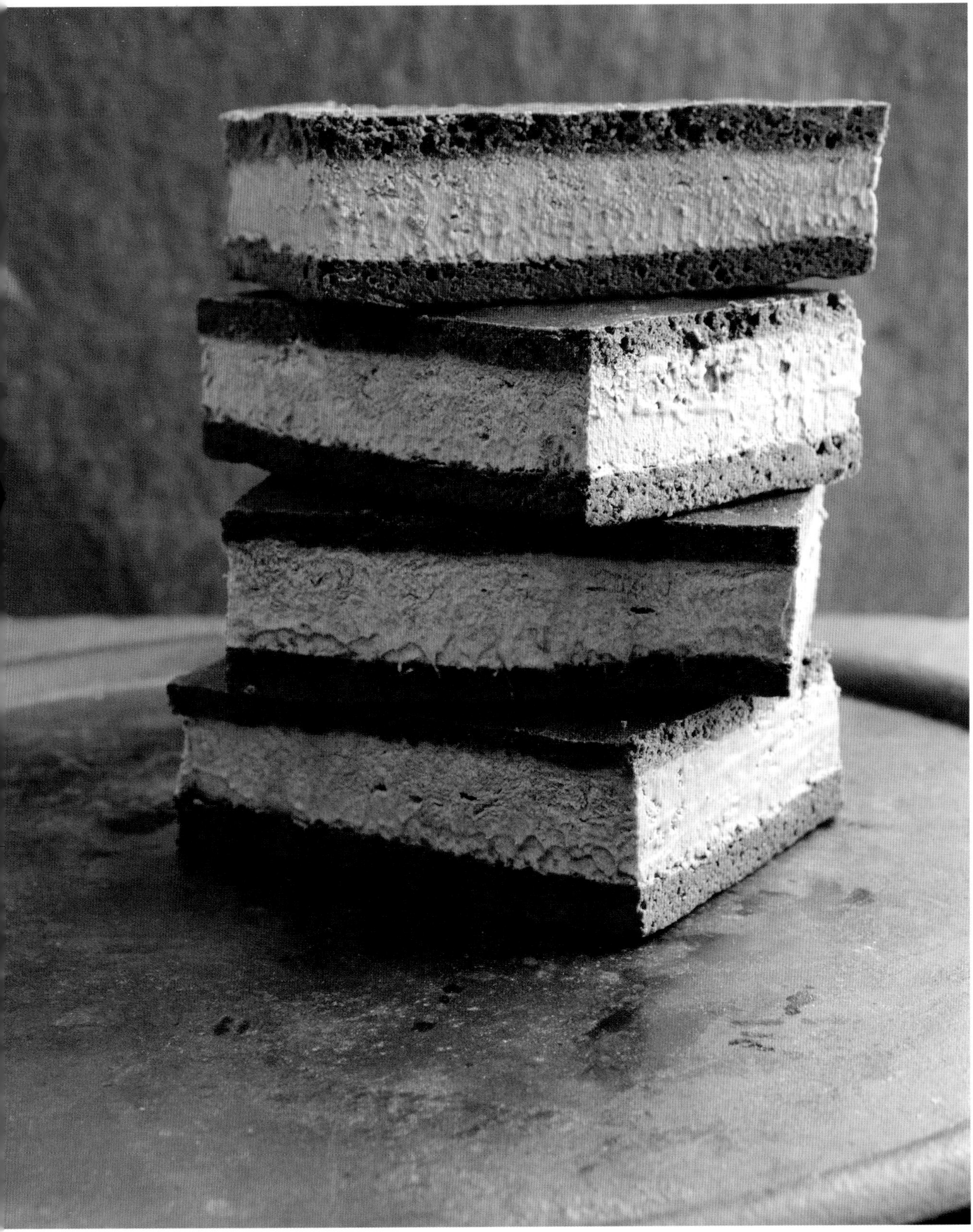

1. Rest a fine-mesh strainer over a medium bowl and set aside.

2. **To make the "ice cream":** Put the cream and chopped mint (if using) in a medium saucepan. Heat the cream over medium heat until it is scalded—that is, small bubbles form on the edges of the cream and it almost, but not quite, comes to a boil. Let it sit for 30 minutes. Strain the cream through the fine-mesh strainer. Pour the cream back in the saucepan and bring back up to just under a boil. Whisk in the peppermint extract (if using instead of fresh mint leaves). Put the chocolate in a medium bowl and pour the hot cream on top. Add the salt and whisk until the chocolate is completely melted. With a rubber spatula, scrape the chocolate mixture into an airtight container and refrigerate overnight.

3. **To make the cake:** Place a rack in the center of the oven and preheat to 350°F [175°C]. Line a 13-by-18-in [33-by-46-cm] rimmed baking sheet with parchment paper, and spray the parchment liberally with nonstick cooking spray. Be sure to spray well; the cake is sticky and you'll have a hard time removing the parchment paper from it if you skip this step.

4. Bring a saucepan filled partway with water to a very gentle simmer over medium-high heat. Place the chocolate in a medium metal or glass bowl. Place the bowl over (not touching) the barely simmering water in the saucepan and heat, stirring occasionally with a wooden spoon or rubber spatula, until the chocolate is completely melted and smooth. Alternatively, microwave the chocolate in a microwave-safe bowl in 30-second intervals, stirring after each interval, until melted and smooth. Whisk the egg yolks, coffee, and salt into the melted chocolate; set aside.

5. Using a stand mixer fitted with the whisk attachment (or with an electric hand mixer), beat the egg whites on medium speed. When they reach the soft-peak stage (that is, when the tines of the whisk leave a trail in the whites, 2 to 3 minutes), watch them carefully until they reach firm-peak stage, which will just take another 30 seconds to a minute. They should hold a peak when you stop the mixer and lift up the whisk attachment slowly from the whites. Using a rubber spatula, fold one-third of the whites into the yolk-chocolate mixture to lighten it, and then gently fold in the rest of the whites. Gently fold in the flour until it is all incorporated.

6. Pour the batter onto the prepared baking sheet. Using an offset spatula, carefully spread the batter evenly to cover the entire baking sheet. Concentrate on spreading the batter towards the corners and the edges of the sheet—the center will be easier to fill once the edges are filled with batter. Don't worry about the top being perfectly smooth; it's more important that the batter be spread evenly so that the cake is the same thickness throughout. Bake for 10 to 12 minutes, or until the top of the cake is firm and dry when you touch it. It may look a bit glossy and wet while baking, but touch it after about 8 minutes to check doneness and continue to test until it is dry to the touch. Let the cake cool in the pan on a wire rack for 20 to 30 minutes. Place the cooled cake in the freezer for at least 30 minutes or up to overnight (in this case, wrapped well with plastic wrap) to make peeling off the parchment easier.

7. Have a sheet of parchment paper ready that is slightly larger than the baked cake surface and set it on a work surface. Remove the cake from the freezer and run a paring knife around the edge of the cake to release it from the sides of the baking sheet. Invert the cake directly onto the sheet of parchment. Carefully peel off the bottom parchment (which is now on top of the cake). Cut the cake in half widthwise, cutting through the parchment underneath as well so you can lift off one half of the cake. Place half of the cake (with parchment underneath) on a baking sheet, cutting board, or large flat platter.

8. Using a stand mixer fitted with the whisk attachment (or with an electric hand mixer or by hand with a whisk), whisk the "ice cream" base on medium speed for 2 to 3 minutes, or until it holds stiff peaks. Use an offset spatula to spread it evenly in a thick layer on top of the cake half that is on the baking sheet. Carefully invert the other half of the cake onto the ice cream base; center it and press it down so it's relatively flat and even. Make room in the freezer for the cake and place the whole thing in the freezer for at least 6 hours or up to overnight.

9. When ready to serve, peel off the parchment on both the top and the bottom of the cake. Using a hot knife, trim the edges of the cake to get a clean edge. You will end up with a rectangle about 8 by 12 in [20 by 30 cm]. Slice the ice cream sandwich cake into 8 pieces, each about 3 by 4 in [8 by 10 cm].

10. Serve immediately, or store in the freezer, wrapped well in plastic wrap, for up to 3 weeks. These are best served after they've been removed from the freezer and set out for 10 to 15 minutes before eating to allow the ice cream to soften.

MOCHA SHAVED ICE

- 170 g/6 oz bittersweet chocolate, finely chopped
- 240 g/1 cup hot brewed strong coffee
- 240 g/1 cup whole milk
- ½ tsp kosher salt
- 2 tsp vanilla extract
- 2 Tbsp Kahlúa or other coffee-flavored liqueur (optional)

VANILLA CREAM

- 240 g/1 cup heavy cream
- 2 tsp vanilla extract

- Approximately 3-in [8-cm] block of bittersweet chocolate, at room temperature, for garnish

MOCHA SHAVED ICE
WITH VANILLA CREAM

If you've ever indulged in affogato—a classic simple Italian dessert in which a scoop of vanilla gelato is doused with a shot of espresso—you'll love this quick and easy variation. Coffee is mixed with chocolate and milk to make a quick frozen ice base; an optional shot of Kahlúa or other coffee-flavored liqueur helps keep the ice a bit softer for easier blending (alcohol lowers the freezing point of ice creams, making for a softer result). You layer scoops of shaved ice with dollops of vanilla-scented soft cream and, as you eat it, the layers meld together and get even creamier—it tastes a little bit like a frozen chocolate cream pie. It's one of my favorite fast treats and I often have some on hand in the freezer for last-minute sweet cravings. The sugar content in the chocolate in this recipe measures about 66 grams, which is about 16 grams per serving.

1. To make the shaved ice: Put the chopped chocolate in a medium bowl. Pour the hot coffee directly on top of the chocolate. Heat the milk in a small saucepan over medium-high heat until it is scalded—that is, small bubbles form on the edges of the milk and it almost, but not quite, comes to a boil. Pour the milk into the chocolate-coffee mixture. Whisk until the chocolate is completely melted. Add the salt, vanilla, and Kahlúa (if using) and stir until combined. Place the shaved ice base in a shallow covered container and freeze overnight.

2. The next day, remove the shaved ice base from the freezer and let sit for 10 to 15 minutes to soften slightly. Use a fork or knife to break up the ice into pieces the size of ice cubes and place in a food processor. Process the ice about 1 minute, or until it becomes a slush. Scrape out into a container and put back in the freezer while you prepare the vanilla cream.

SERVES

4

Continued

3. To make the vanilla cream: Using a stand mixer fitted with the whisk attachment (or with an electric hand mixer or by hand with a whisk), whip the heavy cream and vanilla on medium speed until the cream holds soft peaks that droop a little when the whisk is lifted.

4. To serve, in tall glasses, mugs, or dessert bowls, alternate layers of shaved ice with spoonfuls of whipped cream, beginning and ending with cream. Using the back of a paring knife or a vegetable peeler, scrape the chocolate block to make choc- olate shavings and scatter them evenly on top of each serving.

5. Store the shaved ice, well covered, in the freezer for up to 3 weeks.

DEEP-DARK-CHOCOLATE PUDDING CAKES

- 280 g/10 oz bittersweet chocolate, finely chopped
- 115 g/½ cup unsalted butter
- 2 large eggs plus 2 egg yolks
- 120 g/½ cup heavy cream
- ½ tsp kosher salt
- 2 tsp vanilla extract
- Unsweetened heavy cream, whipped to soft peaks, for garnish

The key to making sure these super-chocolate-y cakes have a soft pudding-like core is to under-bake them ever so slightly, so that when you break into them with a fork, the centers are molten and gooey. Keep a careful eye on them; you want the centers to still be soft and wobbly when you take them out of the oven. I like to offset the richness of the cake with a little dollop of unsweetened whipped cream. There are about 110 grams of sugar total (just over ½ cup) in the chocolate in this recipe; each pudding cake contains about 18 grams of sugar.

1. Place a rack in the center of the oven and preheat to 350°F [175°C]. Butter six 4-oz [120-ml] ramekins.

2. Bring a saucepan filled partway with water to a very gentle simmer over medium-high heat. Place the chocolate and butter in a medium metal or glass bowl. Place the bowl over (not touching) the barely simmering water in the saucepan and heat, stirring occasionally, until the chocolate and butter are completely melted and smooth. Alternatively, microwave the chocolate and butter in a microwave-safe bowl in 30-second intervals, stirring after each interval, until melted and smooth. In a large bowl, by hand with a whisk, whip the eggs and egg yolks. Whip in the heavy cream, salt, and vanilla. Whisk in the chocolate mixture until thoroughly combined.

3. Divide the batter evenly among the prepared ramekins and place on a baking sheet. Bake for 16 to 20 minutes, or until the outsides of the cakes start to set and feel firm to the touch and the insides are still wiggly and soft when you poke them in the center. Remove the cakes from the oven and let them sit for a few minutes to firm up.

4. Run a knife around the cakes and carefully invert onto serving plates. Serve immediately with a little unsweetened whipped cream.

MAKES

6

INDIVIDUAL CAKES

DARK CHOCOLATE MOUSSE

- 360 g/1½ cups heavy cream
- 100 g/3½ oz bittersweet chocolate, finely chopped
- Pinch of kosher salt

PÂTE BRISÉE

- 140 g/1 cup all-purpose flour
- ¼ tsp kosher salt
- 130 g/9 Tbsp cold unsalted butter, cut into 9 pieces
- 1 egg yolk
- 2 Tbsp cold whole milk

CHOCOLATE TRUFFLE FILLING

- 180 g/¾ cup heavy cream
- 120 g/½ cup whole milk
- 250 g/9 oz bittersweet chocolate, finely chopped
- 2 egg yolks
- 2 Tbsp unsalted butter
- ½ tsp kosher salt

- Approximately 3-in [8-cm] block of bittersweet chocolate, at warm room temperature, for garnish

TRUFFLE CHOCOLATE CREAM PIE

Unbelievably, this rich, decadent pie contains no added sugar. Our workhorse recipe for flaky pie dough makes a perfect crust for the double chocolate layers. One is creamy light mousse and the other, a dense, chocolate-rich truffle base. The total amount of sugar in the chocolate in this recipe clocks in at around 140 grams (about ¾ cup), or about 18 grams of sugar per slice of pie.

1. To make the mousse: Heat the cream in a small saucepan over medium heat until it is scalded—that is, small bubbles form on the edges of the cream and it almost, but not quite, comes to a boil. Place the chocolate in a medium bowl and pour the hot cream on top. Add the salt and whisk until the chocolate is completely melted. With a rubber spatula, scrape the chocolate mixture into an airtight container and refrigerate overnight.

2. To make the pâte brisée: Using a stand mixer fitted with the paddle attachment (or with an electric hand mixer), beat the flour and salt for 10 to 15 seconds, or until mixed. Add the butter and beat slowly for 45 to 60 seconds, or just until the flour is no longer bright white, holds together when you clump it, and there are still lumps of butter the size of a pecan throughout. In a small bowl, whisk together the egg yolk and milk and add all at once to the flour-butter mixture. Beat very briefly on low speed for 20 to 30 seconds, *just* until it barely comes together. It will look really shaggy and more like a mess than a dough.

Continued

MAKES

ONE

9-IN [23-CM] PIE

3. Dump the dough out onto a work surface and gather it into a tight mound. Using the heel of your hand, smear the dough, starting at the top of the mound and sliding your palm down the sides of the mound along the work surface, until most of the butter chunks are smeared into the dough and the whole thing comes together. (This technique is called *fraisage* and makes for a very flaky pie dough.) Wrap the dough tightly in plastic wrap and press it down to make a flattened disk. Refrigerate for at least 1 hour before using. The dough can be stored in the refrigerator for up to 4 days (wrapped in another layer of plastic wrap if storing for more than 1 day) or in the freezer for up to 4 weeks.

4. Remove the pastry dough from the refrigerator and knead it slightly to make it malleable if it feels stiff. Using a rolling pin, press the dough to flatten it into a disk about 1/2 in [1 cm] thick. Generously flour your work surface and the dough disk. Carefully roll out the disk into a circle about 12 in [30 cm] in diameter. Make sure the table you are rolling on is well floured so that the dough does not stick to it; likewise make sure the disk itself is floured well enough to keep your rolling pin from sticking to it. Roll from the center of the disk outward and gently rotate the disk a quarter turn after each roll to ensure that the disk gets stretched out evenly into a nice circle. Don't worry if the dough breaks a bit, especially towards the edges. You can easily patch these tears up once you've lined your pie plate.

5. Once the dough circle is about 12 in [30 cm] in diameter, roll it gently around the rolling pin and then unfurl it on top of a 9-in [13-cm] aluminum or glass pie plate. Press the dough gently into the bottom and sides of the plate, leaving a 1/2-in [1-cm] lip around the edge (to allow for shrinkage in the oven), and using any scraps or odd pieces to patch up any tears or missing bits.

6. Refrigerate the pie shell for at least 30 minutes. (The gluten needs a little time to relax so it doesn't shrink as much in the oven). The unbaked pie shell can be stored, tightly wrapped in plastic wrap, in the refrigerator for up to 3 days or in the freezer for up to 4 weeks. If frozen, the pie shell can be baked directly from the freezer.

7. Place a rack in the center of the oven and preheat to 350°F [175°C].

8. Blind bake (that is, prebake) the shell so it doesn't get soggy when you eventually fill it: Line the shell with parchment paper or a large coffee filter and then fill it with pie weights, uncooked beans, uncooked rice, or even well-washed marble-size rocks. Press down slightly on the weights to make sure the shell is entirely filled and place in the oven. Bake for 30 to 35 minutes, or until the shell is brown on the edges and pale and matte when you lift the parchment and peek at the surface of the shell. (If the edges brown too quickly, cover the shell loosely with foil.) When the pie shell is done blind baking, remove it from the oven and let cool on a wire rack. When the pie shell has cooled, remove the parchment paper and pie weights.

9. To make truffle filling: Heat the cream and milk in a small saucepan over medium heat until scalded—that is, small bubbles form on the edges of the mixture and it almost, but not quite, comes to a boil. Place the chopped chocolate in a medium bowl and pour the hot cream mixture on top. Whisk until the chocolate is completely melted. Whisk in the egg yolks, butter, and salt until completely mixed. Pour into the baked pie shell and bake for 25 to 35 minutes, or until the filling is set and jiggles slowly like Jell-O when you wiggle it. Remove the pie from the oven and let cool on a wire rack to room temperature for about 2 hours or until completely cooled.

10. Remove the mousse from the refrigerator. Using a stand mixer fitted with the whisk attachment (or with an electric hand mixer or by hand with a whisk), whip the mousse on medium speed for 2 to 3 minutes, or until it holds stiff peaks—that is, when you lift the whisk out of the mousse, the mousse stands tall and holds its shape. Scrape the whipped mousse on top of the cooled truffle filling and spread evenly with a rubber spatula or a wooden spoon.

11. Using the back of a paring knife or a vegetable peeler, scrape the chocolate block to make chocolate shavings and scatter them evenly on top of the pie. Slice the pie with a thin knife dipped in hot water and serve immediately. The pie can be stored, in an airtight container or covered loosely with plastic wrap, in the refrigerator for up to 4 days.

CHAPTER THREE

USING HONEY

Honey is a terrific all-natural way to add sweetness to desserts with fewer of the potential side effects of consuming too much refined white sugar. It contains nutrients and antioxidants (sugar is devoid of both), is more readily digestible to our systems, and has a lower glycemic index than sugar, allowing us to consume it with less of a blood sugar increase. And it's delicious! We've been eating honey since ancient times, both as food and as medicine. The treats in this chapter are unbelievably good and you won't miss the sugar once you taste the warm, mellow flavor honey brings to these desserts.

BUN DOUGH

- 240 g/1 cup water, at body temperature (when you put your finger in it, it should feel neither cold nor hot)
- ½ tsp active dry yeast or 3 g/ 0.1 oz fresh cake yeast
- 350 g/2½ cups unbleached all-purpose flour, plus up to about 35 g/¼ cup more, if needed
- 1¼ tsp kosher salt
- 50 g/¼ cup olive oil or other mild vegetable oil

HONEY GOO

- 115 g/½ cup unsalted butter
- 170 g/½ cup honey
- 120 g/½ cup heavy cream
- 120 g/½ cup water
- ¼ tsp kosher salt

BUN FILLING

- 240 g/2 cups raw unsalted cashews, chopped
- 115 g/½ cup unsalted butter, very soft
- 2 tsp ground cinnamon

MAKES

12

BUNS

HONEY CASHEW MORNING BUNS

Our famous sticky bun at Flour is unapologetically sweet. It's drenched in a brown sugar-honey "goo" and chock-full of cinnamon sugar and pecans. Not only did it beat Bobby Flay in a *Throwdown* episode on the Food Network, he also graciously picked it as his choice for *The Best Thing I Ever Ate* in another TV show. It has become a signature item, and it has put us on the map.

I confess that I can only eat a few bites and then I'm done. It's incredibly rich, which is what makes it so good, but I longed for something just as decadent but in a lighter, less sugary way. These morning buns are the answer. Made with a light, yeasted, unsweetened dough, they get filled with chopped cashews (my favorite nut) and then baked in a honey goo that is rich with cream and butter, and sweet with a little honey, but not so much that they hide the flavor of the bun or cashew. I especially love the caramelized pieces on the edge of the pan.

1. To make the dough: Lightly oil a large bowl.

2. Using a stand mixer fitted with the dough hook attachment, combine the water and yeast and let sit for 20 to 30 seconds to allow the yeast to dissolve and activate. Dump the flour and salt onto the yeast mixture, and carefully turn on the mixer on low speed. Let the dough mix for about 10 seconds. (To prevent the flour from flying out of the bowl, turn the mixer on and off several times until the flour is mixed into the liquid, and then keep it on low speed.) When the dough is still shaggy looking, drizzle in the olive oil, aiming it along the side of the work bowl to keep it from splashing and making a mess.

3. With the mixer still on low speed, knead the dough for 4 to 5 minutes, or until it is smooth and supple. The dough should be somewhat sticky but still smooth, and have an elastic, stretchy consistency. If it is much stiffer than this, mix in 2 to 3 Tbsp water; if it is much looser than this, mix in 2 to 3 Tbsp flour.

Continued

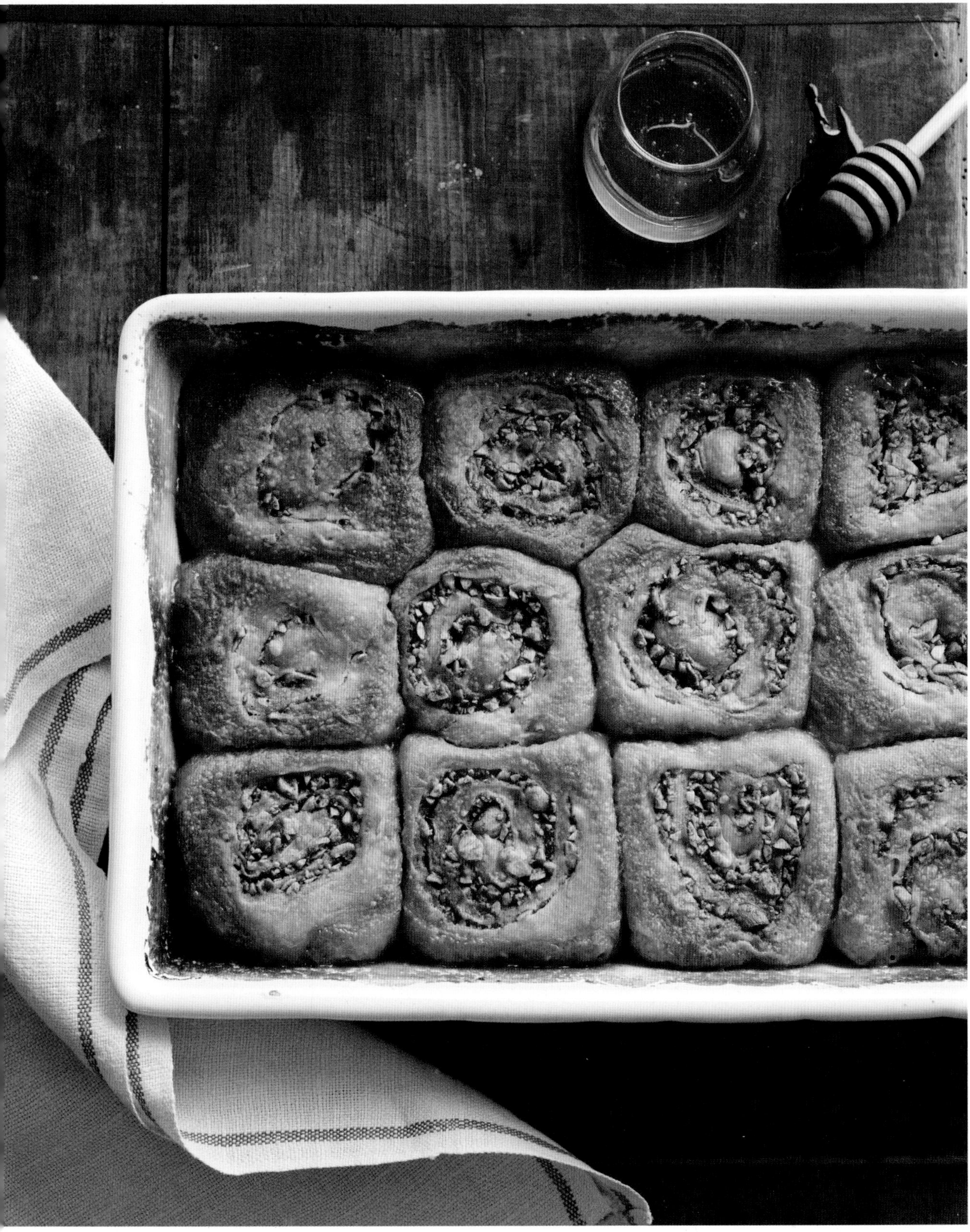

4. Transfer the dough to the oiled bowl. Cover the bowl with a piece of plastic wrap or a damp lint-free cloth. Place the bowl in a draft-free, warm place (78 to 82°F [25 to 28°C] is ideal; an area near the stove or in the oven with only the pilot light on is good) for 2 to 3 hours. The dough should rise until it is about double in bulk. (This is called proofing the dough.)

5. Meanwhile, make the honey goo: In a medium saucepan, melt the butter over medium heat and whisk in the honey, cream, water, and salt. Remove the pan from the heat and let the goo cool for about 30 minutes before using, or until room temperature. The goo can be stored in an airtight container in the refrigerator for up to 2 weeks.

6. To make the filling: Place a rack in the center of the oven and preheat to 350°F [175°C]. Put the cashews on a baking sheet and toast for 8 to 10 minutes, or until lightly toasted. Turn off the oven and set the cashews aside to cool.

7. Punch down the dough to deflate it—literally give it a punch in the center of the puffy dough, which will allow you to roll it out more easily. On a floured work surface, roll out the dough into a 12-in [30-cm] square about ¼ in [6 mm] thick. It will be a bit stretchy and it may spring back, but keep rolling gently until it roughly holds its shape.

8. In a small bowl, with a wooden spoon, mix together the butter, cinnamon, and cashews. Spread this mixture evenly over the entire surface of the dough square.

9. Using your hands and starting from the top of the square, and working your way down, roll the dough loosely like a jelly roll until the entire sheet is rolled up. Using a sharp knife, trim both edges of the dough roll about ¼ in [6 mm] to even out the ends. Using a bench scraper or a chef's knife, cut the roll into 12 equal pieces, each about

1 in [3 cm] thick. (At this point, the unbaked buns can be tightly wrapped in plastic wrap—either individually or stack them all and wrap as a tower—and frozen for up to 1 week. When ready to bake, remove the buns from the freezer. Leave them wrapped and thaw in the refrigerator over-night, or at room temperature for 2 to 3 hours; proceed as directed.)

10. Pour the goo into a 9-by-13 in [23-by-33 cm] baking pan. Place the buns in the pan, evenly spaced. If some of the buns have become oblong or oddly shaped from the cutting and moving around, feel free to arrange them once they are in the pan into round spirals. Cover the pan loosely with plastic wrap and let the buns proof at warm room temperature (78 to 82°F [25 to 28°C] is ideal; an area near the stove or in the oven with only the pilot light on is good) for 1 to 2 hours, or until the dough is puffy, pillowy, and soft and the buns are touching.

11. About 15 minutes before the buns are ready to bake, place a rack in the center of the oven and preheat to 400°F [205°C].

12. Bake for 40 to 50 minutes, or until the buns are pale and light golden brown. Remove from the oven and let cool in the pan on a wire rack for 10 to 20 minutes.

13. Using a spatula, invert the buns, one at a time, onto a serving platter. Serve warm. (These are best served warm or within 4 hours of baking. You could make them one day and serve them the next after warming them in a 300°F [150°C] oven for 6 to 8 minutes.)

CHERRY ALMOND GRANOLA

- 180 g/1½ cups dried cherries (unsweetened if possible)
- 100 g/½ cup vegetable oil, such as canola
- 85 g/¼ cup honey
- 1 tsp vanilla extract
- 150 g/1½ cups slivered almonds
- 50 g/½ cup almond flour
- 150 g/1½ cups old-fashioned rolled oats (not instant or quick cooking)
- 60 g/¾ cup unsweetened shredded coconut
- 1 tsp kosher salt
- 1 tsp ground cinnamon
- 40 g/¼ cup flaxseed
- 35 g/¼ cup sunflower seeds
- 50 g/¼ cup millet
- 35 g/¼ cup sesame seeds

When I was testing the recipe for the Nutty-Seedy-Fruity Energy Bars (page 100), I went through several iterations to get the right proportion of nuts, honey, fruits, and spices. What stayed consistent throughout all of the trial batches was how much I loved the edge pieces of the bars—the bits that didn't quite meld together to form a bar, but instead baked up brown and crunchy. Thus—this granola! It's full of almonds and cherries and bound together with just enough honey to make it slightly sweet. It's fantastic on its own as a snack or mixed into yogurt for a super-healthy, delicious breakfast.

1. Place a rack in the center of the oven and preheat to 325°F [165°C]. Line a baking sheet with parchment paper. Spray the parchment with nonstick cooking spray.

2. Put the dried cherries in a medium bowl and pour boiling water over the fruit to cover. Let sit for 30 minutes.

3. In a small bowl, combine the vegetable oil, honey, and vanilla. In a large bowl, combine the almonds, almond flour, oats, coconut, salt, cinnamon, flaxseed, sunflower seeds, millet, and sesame seeds. Using a wooden spoon, add the wet ingredients to the dry ingredients and stir well until thoroughly combined.

4. Drain the cherries into a bowl, reserving 2 Tbsp of the soaking water and discarding the rest of the liquid. Divide the cherries roughly in half, place half in a food processor or blender, and add the reserved soaking water. Process until you have a chunky jam. Add the jam to the nut mixture along with the remaining whole cherries. Stir well to combine.

5. Spread the mixture evenly on the prepared baking sheet. Bake for about 20 minutes, stirring the granola a few times to ensure even baking. Turn off the oven and leave the granola in the oven for at least 6 hours or up to overnight. Remove the granola from the oven and break it apart into pieces. The granola can be stored in an airtight container at room temperature for up to 2 weeks or in the freezer for up to 3 months.

MAKES ABOUT

8

CUPS

- 150 g/1½ cups walnuts, coarsely chopped
- 3 large eggs
- 225 g/⅔ cup honey
- 1 Tbsp vanilla extract
- 2 Tbsp finely grated orange zest
- 315 g/2¼ cups all-purpose flour
- 1 tsp baking powder
- ¼ tsp kosher salt
- 120 g/1 cup dried cranberries

CRANBERRY-ORANGE-WALNUT BISCOTTI

Traditional Italian biscotti are meant to be super-hard and dry, perfect for dunking into an espresso and adding a bit of sweetness to your afternoon break. Here in America, we've taken that tradition and made it ours by adding butter and sometimes oil to the dough and generally making the cookies sweeter, softer, and richer. *Mamma mia!* What would the Italians think! I tried to split the difference here: these biscotti do not have additional fat, keeping it in line with tradition, but the use of honey as the sweetener helps soften the dough, resulting in a lighter, crunchier cookie. The walnuts, cranberries, and bright orange combine to make a delightful treat that will become your new family favorite—it quickly became the favorite of many of my recipe testers!

1. Place a rack in the center of the oven and preheat to 325°F [165°C]. Line a baking sheet with parchment paper.

2. Put the walnuts on the prepared baking sheet and toast for 8 to 10 minutes, or until lightly toasted. Set aside to cool.

3. Using a stand mixer fitted with the whisk attachment (or with an electric hand mixer or by hand with a whisk), whisk together the eggs, honey, vanilla, and orange zest on medium-high speed for 1 to 2 minutes, or until well combined.

4. In a large bowl, combine the flour, baking powder, salt, walnuts, and dried cranberries. Pour the egg mixture into the dry ingredients and, using a wooden spoon, mix the two together for 2 to 3 minutes, or until thoroughly combined into a thick dough. You may need to switch to mixing the dough with your hands since the batter can get stiff.

MAKES

15 TO 18

BISCOTTI

5. Dump the dough onto the prepared baking sheet and pat it out into a log about 5 in [13 cm] wide, 12 in [30 cm] long, and 1 in [3 cm] high. It's helpful to wet your hands in a bowl of cold water as you're shaping the log so they won't stick to the dough.

6. Bake the log for 40 to 50 minutes, or until completely browned and firm. Check it by pressing a finger firmly into the middle—it should not give at all. Remove the log from the oven and let it cool on the baking sheet for about 30 minutes, or until it is cool enough to handle comfortably. Decrease the oven temperature to 200°F [95°C].

7. Transfer the log to a cutting board. Using a serrated knife, slice the log on the diagonal into biscotti that are ½ in [1 cm] thick. You should get 15 to 18 biscotti. (At this point, you can store the once-baked biscotti in the freezer, tightly wrapped in plastic wrap, for up to 1 month.)

8. Arrange the biscotti on the baking sheet, with a cut-side down, and bake for 3 to 4 hours, or until the biscotti are completely baked through. Test by poking at the middle of one of the cookies; it should be completely hard. Turn off the oven and leave the biscotti in the oven overnight. Remove the biscotti from the oven.

9. Biscotti can be stored in an airtight container at room temperature for up to 2 weeks.

- 75 g/¾ cup walnuts, coarsely chopped
- 75 g/¾ cup slivered almonds
- 75 g/¾ cup pecan pieces
- 40 g/½ cup dried apple slices, chopped
- 60 g/½ cup dried cranberries
- 60 g/½ cup dried apricots, diced
- 60 g/½ cup sultanas (golden raisins)
- 60 g/½ cup raisins
- 50 g/½ cup almond flour
- 60 g/½ cup buckwheat flour
- 100 g/1 cup old-fashioned rolled oats (not instant or quick cooking)
- 40 g/½ cup unsweetened shredded coconut
- 1 tsp kosher salt
- 1 tsp ground cinnamon
- 100 g/½ cup vegetable oil, such as canola
- 115 g/⅓ cup honey
- 1 super-ripe banana, mashed (optional)
- 40 g/¼ cup flaxseed
- 35 g/¼ cup sunflower seeds
- 50 g/¼ cup millet

NUTTY-SEEDY-FRUITY ENERGY BARS

With all of the tasting I do during the day, I rarely find myself hungry, but I often worry that I'm not eating as well as I should. (I guess that's what happens when you eat Breton butter cakes and *brioche au chocolat* for breakfast, brownie scraps and Boston cream pie trimmings and banana bread bites for lunch, and apple cake edges and muffin tops for afternoon snacks.) Even our granola bar, touted by many to be a healthy choice for a snack, is laden with butter and sugar, making it better suited as an occasional indulgence than a really-healthy-and-good-for-you daily treat.

These bars fit the bill for something sweet and indulgent tasting yet full of nuts and dried fruits and good-for-you grains. It's gluten free as well if you source your oats from a gluten-free company (oats themselves are gluten free but most companies process wheat with the same machines that process the oats, cross-contaminating them). I tested these way more times than I needed to simply because I loved having them on hand as a wonderful way to get a quick, healthy energy boost. I tried them with and without the banana (the banana makes a moister bar with a sweeter flavor), and I changed up the nuts and fruits based on what I had in-house. Play around with what suits you; you won't regret having extras on hand as you test.

1. Place a rack in the center of the oven and preheat to 350°F [175°C].

2. Put the walnuts, almonds, and pecans on a baking sheet and toast for 8 to 10 minutes, or until lightly toasted. Set aside to cool.

3. Put the dried apples, cranberries, apricots, sultanas, and raisins in a medium bowl and pour boiling water over the fruit to cover. Let sit for 30 minutes.

Continued

MAKES

16

BARS

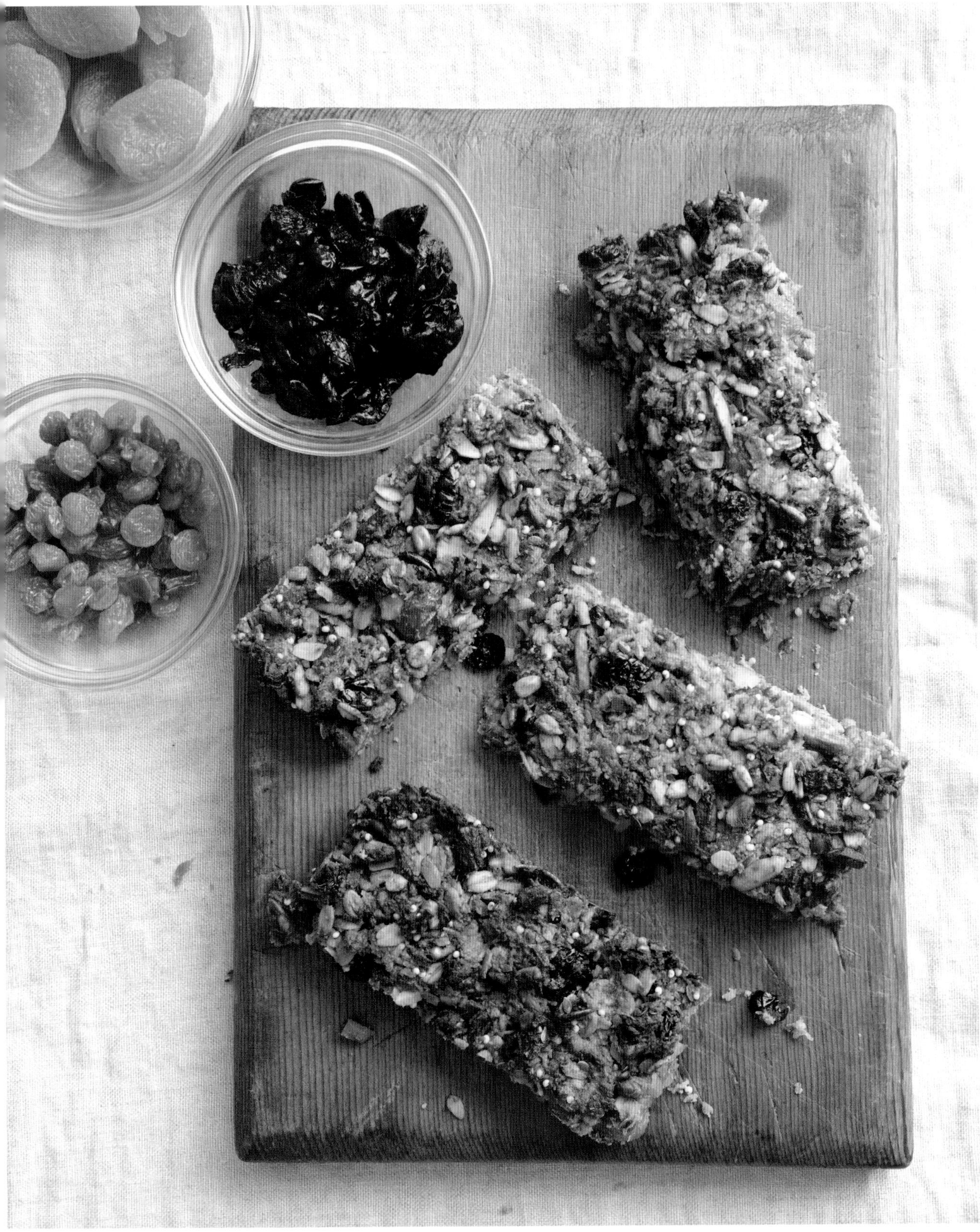

4. Decrease the oven temperature to 325°F [165°C]. Line a baking sheet with parchment paper.

5. In a large bowl, combine the nuts, almond flour, buckwheat flour, oats, coconut, salt, cinnamon, vegetable oil, honey, banana (if using), flaxseed, sunflower seeds, and millet. Using a wooden spoon, stir well until thoroughly combined.

6. Drain the fruit into a medium bowl, reserving ¼ cup [60 ml] of the soaking water and discarding the rest of the liquid. Divide the fruit roughly in half, place half in a food processor or in a blender, and add the reserved soaking water. Process until you have a chunky jam. Add the jam to the nut mixture along with the remaining whole fruit. Stir well to combine.

7. Press the mixture evenly on the prepared baking sheet into a rectangle about 12 by 8 in [30 by 20 cm]. Using a sharp knife, cut the rectangle in half lengthwise and then cut each half into 8 pieces widthwise so you have a total of 16 bars. Bake for 35 to 45 minutes, or until golden brown throughout. Reduce the oven temperature to 250°F [120°C] and continue to bake for another hour. Turn off the oven and let the bars sit in the oven until completely cool. They will get pretty dark, but that is okay.

8. Remove from the oven and, using a sharp knife, recut the bars along the marks to separate (they will have joined slightly during baking). The bars can be stored in an airtight container at room temperature for up to 1 week.

BANANA CINNAMON BREAD PUDDING

- 960 g/4 cups half-and-half
- 1 tsp ground cinnamon
- ¼ tsp kosher salt
- 225 g/⅔ cup honey
- 3 large eggs plus 4 egg yolks
- 3 super-ripe bananas, mashed (really ripe—I mean it! Black and spotty on the outside and soft and sweet on the inside)
- 6 cups bread cubes, either with or without crusts, about 1 in [3 cm] cubed (weight will depend on type of bread used; we use day-old white bread)
- Unsweetened heavy cream, whipped to soft peaks, for garnish

We bake so much bread for our sandwiches at the bakery that we are constantly trying to come up with fun, creative ways to use up the bread ends: We give them away with soup, we cut them into croutons, we bag them up and sell huge bags of ends for about a buck-and-a-half (best deal in town!). Making bread pudding is my favorite use for the extra bread. This one is filled with naturally sweet bananas, a touch of cinnamon, and honey to round it out. I love eating it warm out of the oven, but I'll admit to also sneaking bites of it straight from the refrigerator— it's that good.

1. Place a rack in the center of the oven and preheat to 350°F [175°C].

2. In a medium bowl, whisk together the half-and-half, cinnamon, salt, honey, eggs, and egg yolks, then whisk in the mashed bananas. Put the bread cubes in a 9-by-13-in [23-by-33-cm] baking pan and pour the liquid ingredients over the bread. Mix the bread well into the custard to ensure everything is well combined.

3. Bake for 40 to 50 minutes, or until the pudding is firm when you press it in the center and it is just starting to brown. Remove from the oven and let cool on a wire rack for 30 to 45 minutes.

4. Using a stand mixer fitted with the whisk attachment (or with an electric hand mixer or by hand with a whisk), whip the cream on medium speed until it holds soft peaks that droop a little when the whisk is lifted.

5. Serve the bread pudding warm, topped with unsweetened softly whipped cream, or store in the refrigerator and serve cold. The bread pudding can be stored, well wrapped with plastic wrap, in the refrigerator for up to 4 days.

SERVES

6 TO 8

- 960 g/4 cups whole milk
- 1 whole cinnamon stick
- 1 vanilla bean, split in half lengthwise
- 100 g/½ cup jasmine or white basmati rice
- 60 g/½ cup currants or raisins
- 3 egg yolks
- 170 g/½ cup honey
- ¼ tsp ground cinnamon
- ¼ tsp kosher salt

VANILLA HONEY RICE PUDDING

In my family, my nickname in Chinese is "Rice Head" because of how much I adore rice. I eat a bowl nightly at dinner and have my entire life. I still remember the first time I learned about rice pudding: my absolute favorite food—rice—combined with my obsession with all things sweet? SCORE! Rice pudding allows me to indulge in rice in an entirely different way. Sweetened with a little honey and currants (feel free to substitute raisins if you don't have currants) and vanilla (don't skimp on this—buy a fresh vanilla bean and it will make a dramatic difference in the end result), it is super simple and crazy delicious. Enjoy this pudding warm or cold.

1. Place the milk and cinnamon stick in a medium saucepan. Using a small paring knife, scrape the seeds from the split vanilla bean into the milk; throw in the pod as well. Bring the milk to a boil over medium-high heat. Stir in the rice with a wooden spoon and decrease the heat to a low simmer. Cook the rice slowly in milk for 20 to 25 minutes, uncovered, or until the rice is soft. Stir regularly during cooking with the wooden spoon to keep the rice from sticking to the bottom.

2. Remove from the heat, remove the cinnamon stick and vanilla bean pod, and stir in the currants. In a medium bowl, whisk together the egg yolks and honey; slowly ladle the hot milk-rice mixture into the yolks, whisking all the while. Continue adding hot milk-rice to the yolks until about half of it is mixed in. (This is called tempering: you are slowly adding hot to cold and gently bringing up the temperature of the cold item to meet the hot.) Dump the rice mixture back into the saucepan and cook over medium heat, stirring constantly with a wooden spoon, for 2 to 3 minutes, or until the mixture thickens. Remove from the heat and stir in the ground cinnamon and salt.

3. Serve warm, or refrigerate and serve cold. The rice pudding can be stored, well wrapped with plastic wrap, in the refrigerator for up to 4 days.

SERVES

3 OR 4

HONEY-CHAMPAGNE SABAYON PARFAITS
WITH FRESH BERRIES

- 8 egg yolks
- 170 g/½ cup honey
- 120 g/½ cup Champagne or other sparkling white wine
- ¼ tsp kosher salt
- 360 g/1½ cups heavy cream
- 260 g/2 cups fresh raspberries
- 260 g/2 cups fresh blackberries
- 260 g/2 cups fresh blueberries

A light, luscious dessert whose sophisticated taste belies the ease in putting it together, this parfait is a perfect dessert to end a summer dinner party. Prepare the parfaits in the afternoon, store them in the refrigerator, and simply pull them out at dessert time to "wows" and "ah-h-h-s." Feel free to vary the fruit. As with most fruit desserts, for the best result, be sure to select the ripest, sweetest fruit.

1. Fill a large bowl with ice.

2. Bring a saucepan filled partway with water to a very gentle simmer over medium-low heat. In a large metal or glass bowl, whisk together the egg yolks, honey, Champagne, and salt. Place the bowl over (not touching) the barely simmering water in the saucepan and heat, whisking constantly, for 10 to 12 minutes, or until thick, light, and lemony colored. When the sabayon has cooked for the proper amount of time, the whisk will leave a trail in the mixture as you are whisking, and you will start to see the bottom of the bowl through the tines of the whisk. Remove the bowl from the heat and set immediately in the bowl of ice. Whisk occasionally over this ice bath for 5 to 8 minutes, or until the sabayon is completely cooled. Remove from the ice bath.

3. Using a stand mixer fitted with the whisk attachment (or with an electric hand mixer or by hand with a whisk), whip the cream on medium speed until it holds stiff peaks that stand up straight when the whisk is lifted. Fold the cream into the sabayon with a rubber spatula. Layer spoonfuls of sabayon with berries in alternate layers in tall Champagne flutes and serve. Parfaits may be made in advance and stored lightly covered in plastic wrap in the refrigerator for 4 to 6 hours. They should be eaten the same day they are made as parfaits don't keep well overnight.

SERVES

6 TO 8

- 300 g/1¼ cups Greek-style whole-milk plain yogurt
- 455 g/3½ cups fresh or frozen raspberries
- 225 g/⅔ cup honey
- 1 Tbsp freshly squeezed lemon juice
- ⅛ tsp kosher salt
- 1 Tbsp vanilla extract

RASPBERRY HONEY FROZEN YOGURT

I have an automatic answer when people ask me what is my favorite dessert of all time: ice cream! I could eat it for breakfast, lunch, and dinner and never tire of it. It makes me inordinately happy. But lately, frozen yogurt has been edging its way into all-time-favorite status. Perhaps it is my maturing taste buds—the tanginess of yogurt is now more interesting to me than the sometimes overly sweet nature of some ice creams. With a lower fat content than ice cream, frozen yogurt is also a bit healthier for me, so I feel okay about consuming it in copious amounts. It's also simpler to make than ice cream and since it typically has fewer ingredients, the flavors of whatever you are churning really shine. This frozen yogurt is a perfect case in point. When Christopher first tasted it, he exclaimed, "This tastes exactly like a bowl of fresh raspberries!" He proceeded to polish off the whole quart, which for me was the best compliment of all.

1. Set a fine-mesh strainer over a medium bowl.

2. Put the yogurt, raspberries, honey, lemon juice, salt, and vanilla in a blender or food processor and blend on high speed for at least 1 minute, or until well mixed. Pour about three-fourths of the mixture through the strainer and, using a rubber spatula, scrape the mixture through to strain out the seeds. Mix the remaining one-fourth of the mixture back into the strained mixture. The final frozen yogurt will have a few seeds, but you won't be overburdened with them.

3. Churn in an ice cream maker according to the manufacturer's directions. When the yogurt has finished churning, transfer it to a storage container and freeze for at least 3 hours to allow it to ripen. During the ripening process, the yogurt becomes harder and smoother and the flavors have a chance to develop. Store the yogurt in an airtight container in the freezer for at least 1 week or up to 1 month. Remove the yogurt from the freezer about 10 minutes before serving to allow it to soften up.

MAKES ABOUT

1

QUART [1 L]

- 140 g/¾ cup unsalted butter, at warm room temperature
- 170 g/½ cup honey
- 1 large egg plus 1 egg yolk, at room temperature
- 1 Tbsp vanilla extract
- 260 g/1 cup unsalted peanut butter with no sugar (ingredients should just read "roasted peanuts")
- 105 g/¾ cup all-purpose flour
- 50 g/½ cup old-fashioned rolled oats (not instant or quick cooking)
- ½ tsp baking soda
- 1¼ tsp kosher salt
- 100 g/¾ cup chopped raw peanuts

MAKES

16 TO 18

COOKIES

PEANUT BUTTER HONEY COOKIES

A scrumptious peanut butter cookie sweetened just with honey was actually one of the more challenging recipes to develop for this book. I started with an unsalted and sugar-free peanut butter. (You'd be surprised at how much sugar your typical jar of Jif or Skippy peanut butter contains.) Honey is the perfect sweetener for peanut butter (who doesn't love a peanut butter and honey sandwich?), but the trick was getting the texture of the cookie just right. Without sugar, the batter has a hard time holding itself together and forming a crunchy, chewy cookie. I adjusted the level of peanut butter, egg, honey, flour, and butter in numerous attempts to keep it from falling apart. Finally my recipe tester Keith came upon the answer: beating each ingredient thoroughly into the batter helped to emulsify the dough enough to hold the cookies together. These cookies aren't traditionally chewy or crispy, but they are soft and cake-like and a super alternative to a sugar-laden peanut butter cookie.

1. Using a stand mixer fitted with the paddle attachment (or with an electric hand mixer), beat the butter on medium speed for 2 minutes, or until it is totally soft and creamy. Decrease the speed to low and add the honey slowly; increase the speed to medium-high and beat until completely creamy and homogenous. If the butter is at all chilled, it will take a long time for this step, so be sure to start with warm room-temperature butter.

2. In a small bowl, whisk together the egg, egg yolk, and vanilla. Slowly add to the butter-honey mixture. Continue to beat on medium-high for 2 minutes; stop the mixer and scrape the bowl well with a rubber spatula. Continue to beat on medium-high for 5 to 7 minutes more, or until the mixture is light and fluffy. (It will look curdled at first but will homogenize and resemble a silky smooth buttercream as the eggs bring it together. If the eggs are at all cold, it will take longer, so be sure to start with room-temperature eggs.)

3. Decrease the speed to low and add the peanut butter. Scrape the bowl and mix for about 30 seconds, or until incorporated. Remove the bowl from the mixer.

4. In a separate bowl, using a rubber spatula or a wooden spoon, mix together the flour, oats, baking soda, salt, and peanuts and stir to combine. Add the dry ingredients to the wet ingredients and, using a rubber spatula, fold by hand until the dry ingredients are thoroughly incorporated. Refrigerate the dough in an airtight container for at least 1 hour or up to several days.

5. Place a rack in the center of the oven and preheat to 350°F [175°C].

6. Using a small ice cream scoop or a rounded spoon, drop the dough in balls the size of a ping-pong ball onto a baking sheet about 2 in [5 cm] apart. Press the dough balls down flat with the palm of your hand and, using a fork, make a traditional criss-cross pattern on the top of the cookies. Bake for 16 to 20 minutes, or until the cookies are golden brown on the edges and just beginning to color in the middle, rotating the baking sheet halfway through baking. Remove the cookies from the oven and let them cool on the sheet for 5 to 10 minutes, then transfer the cookies to a wire rack to cool completely. Don't be tempted to move them until they are set up or they will break. The cookies can be stored in an airtight container at room temperature for up to 5 days.

- 60 g/½ cup sultanas (golden raisins)
- 5 or 6 medium Empire, McIntosh, Golden Delicious, Gala, or other sweet baking apples, peeled, cored, and sliced ¼ in [6 mm] thick
- 85 g/¼ cup honey
- ½ tsp ground cinnamon
- ⅛ tsp kosher salt

CRUMB TOPPING

- 100 g/1 cup old-fashioned rolled oats (not instant or quick cooking)
- 105 g/¾ cup all-purpose flour
- 1 tsp ground cinnamon
- ½ tsp kosher salt
- 115 g/½ cup unsalted butter, melted and cooled
- 85 g/¼ cup honey
- 1 Tbsp vanilla extract

- Unsweetened heavy cream, whipped to soft peaks, for garnish

SERVES

6 TO 8

WARM APPLE-RAISIN CRISP

Crisps, sadly, can sometimes be anything but. I've slogged my way through soggy crisps, gummy crisps, and mushy crisps, making me wonder how they got their name. In this dessert we sweeten the crisp topping with a little honey, and the apples and raisins themselves are sweet enough to barely need any additional sweetener. But the absence of sugar in the topping means it can tend more towards the chewy than the crispy. We get around that by baking the topping first on its own so it has some time to dry out and get a little crunchy. For those of you who are experienced pie bakers, think of this as "blind baking" the topping before adding it to the apples. In so doing you'll get a crispy apple crisp that is deserving of its name. (For a fabulous gluten-free version, substitute 70 g/½ cup brown rice flour and 85 g/¼ cup potato starch for the 105 g/¾ cup all-purpose flour.)

1. Place a rack in the center of the oven and preheat to 350°F [175°C].

2. Put the golden raisins in a small bowl and pour boiling water over the raisins to cover. Let sit for 1 hour. Drain the raisins and discard the soaking water.

3. In a large bowl, combine the apples, raisins, honey, cinnamon, and salt and toss to coat. Place the apple mixture in an 8-in [20-cm] or 9-in [23-cm] baking pan with a 2-qt [2-L] capacity.

4. To make the topping: In the same bowl used for mixing the apples, with a wooden spoon, mix together the oats, flour, cinnamon, and salt until evenly combined. In a small bowl, whisk together the butter, honey, and vanilla; drizzle over the crumb topping and mix until well incorporated.

Continued

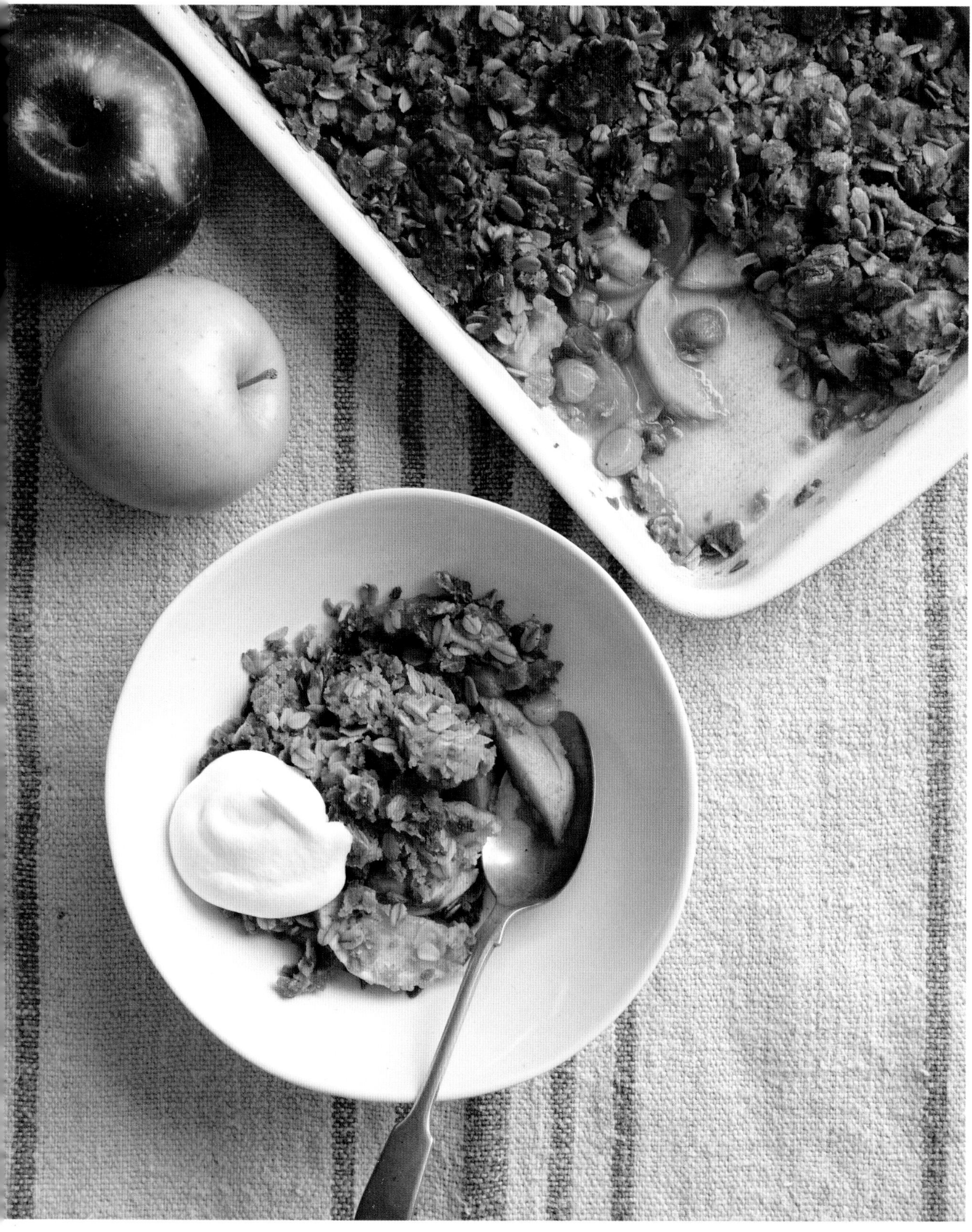

5. Spread the crumb topping on an ungreased baking sheet and bake for about 15 minutes, or until the topping just barely starts to brown and dry a bit. Remove from the oven and, using a spatula or spoon, carefully scrape the topping from the baking sheet and sprinkle evenly over the apples. Bake for 40 to 50 minutes, or until the topping is crispy and deep golden brown and the apples are tender. Let cool on a wire rack for at least 30 minutes before serving with whipped cream alongside. The crisp can be stored, well wrapped with plastic wrap, in the refrigerator for up to 3 days. To serve, rewarm in a 300°F [150°C] oven for 10 to 15 minutes.

PAIN D'ÉPICES

I first made *pain d'épices*—a classic French honey cake—when I was the pastry chef at Rialto in Cambridge, MA, teaching myself pastry by going through *The International Dictionary of Desserts, Pastries, and Confections*, by Carole Bloom. The cake gets its flavor from the mellow honey and panoply of spices. I'll admit that it took some time before the blend of anise, nutmeg, and cloves appealed to me. Not having grown up with many of these flavors, I wasn't used to their licorice-y sharp bite. In this cake they meld beautifully, and it's a lovely treat to have on hand for snacking during the colder winter months. You'll make it over and over—a loaf never lasts as long as I think it will because it's hard to resist stealing small tastes throughout the day.

- 2 Tbsp unsalted butter, melted and cooled, plus softened butter for serving
- 170 g/½ cup honey
- 120 g/½ cup whole milk, at room temperature
- 1 Tbsp finely grated orange zest
- 1 large egg plus egg yolk
- 165 g/1 cup whole-wheat flour
- 1 tsp baking powder
- ½ tsp ground anise seed
- ¼ tsp freshly ground pepper
- ½ tsp freshly grated nutmeg
- ½ tsp ground cinnamon
- ¼ tsp ground ginger
- ¼ tsp ground cloves
- ¼ tsp kosher salt

1. Place a rack in the center of the oven and preheat to 350°F [175°C]. Butter and flour a 9-by-5-in [23-by-13-cm] loaf pan, or butter and line the bottom and sides with parchment paper.

2. In a small bowl, whisk together the butter, honey, milk, and orange zest. Whisk in the egg and egg yolk until well combined. In a large bowl, stir together the flour, baking powder, anise, pepper, nutmeg, cinnamon, ginger, cloves, and salt. Pour the wet ingredients into the dry ingredients and, with a rubber spatula, fold to combine well.

3. Scrape the batter into the prepared pan. Bake for 35 to 45 minutes, or until the cake springs back when you press it in the center with your finger. Remove from the oven and let cool in the pan on a wire rack for 30 to 40 minutes until you can pop it out of the pan. Serve warm with a little bit of softened butter. *Pain d'épices* may be stored for up to 3 days at room temperature, well wrapped, or up to a month in the freezer. Remove from the freezer and thaw overnight at room temperature. Slice and toast lightly before serving.

MAKES

ONE

9-IN [23-CM] LOAF

- Pâte Brisée (see page 88)
- 3 ripe medium peaches
- 225 g/8 oz whole-milk ricotta cheese
- 60 g/¼ cup crème fraîche (see page 24) or whole-milk plain yogurt
- 85 g/4 Tbsp honey
- 1 large egg plus 2 egg yolks
- 1 tsp vanilla extract
- ⅛ tsp kosher salt
- 1 Tbsp finely grated lemon zest
- 1 Tbsp water

FRESH PEACH RICOTTA TART

When you become a pastry chef you spend so much time baking at work that often you don't bake that much at home. My pastry chef Sarah is an exception: after a full day of making cake batters, rolling tart shells, and piping buttercream, she goes home and bakes another set of desserts for her family and friends. She brought a scrumptious baked ricotta tart into work one day, and I adapted it here using only honey to sweeten the tart. The fresh peaches meld marvelously with the ricotta, making an excellent, beautiful dessert.

1. First, make the tart shell using a 10-in [25-cm] tart ring or a fluted tart pan. Remove the pastry dough from the refrigerator and knead it slightly to make it malleable if it feels stiff. Using a rolling pin, press the dough to flatten it into a disk about ½ in [1 cm] thick. Generously flour your work surface and the dough disk. Carefully roll out the disk into a circle about 12 in [30 cm] in diameter. Make sure the table you are rolling on is well floured so that the dough does not stick to it; likewise, make sure the disk itself is floured well enough to keep your rolling pin from sticking to it. Roll from the center of the disk outward and gently rotate the disk a quarter turn after each roll to ensure that the disk gets stretched out evenly into a nice circle. Don't worry if the dough breaks a bit, especially towards the edges. You can easily patch these tears once you've lined your shell.

2. Once the dough circle is about 12 in [30 cm] in diameter, roll it gently around the rolling pin and then unfurl it on top of the tart ring. Press the dough to the bottom and sides of the tart ring, taking care to press the dough into the bottom edge of the pan, and use any scraps or odd pieces to patch any tears or missing bits. Make sure that the entire tart ring is well covered with dough, and press one last time all the way around to ensure that any holes have been patched. Using a small paring knife or scissors, trim the dough a little higher than the ring as it will shrink a bit when it bakes.

MAKES

10-IN [25-CM] TART

3. Refrigerate the tart shell for at least 30 minutes. (The gluten needs a little time to relax so it doesn't shrink as much in the oven.) The unbaked pie shell can be stored, tightly wrapped in plastic wrap, in the refrigerator for up to 3 days or in the freezer for up to 4 weeks. If frozen, the pie shell can be baked directly from the freezer.

4. Place a rack in the center of the oven and preheat to 350°F [175°C].

5. Blind-bake (that is, prebake) the shell so it doesn't get soggy when you eventually fill it: Line the tart shell with parchment paper or a large coffee filter and then fill it with pie weights, uncooked beans, uncooked rice, or even well-washed marble-size rocks. Press down slightly on the weights to make sure the shell is entirely filled and place in the oven. Bake for 20 to 25 minutes, or until the entire shell is matte and no longer looks like raw dough. (If the edges brown too quickly, cover the shell loosely with foil.) It doesn't need to fully color at this point; we are just trying to give the shell a head start in baking before we fill it with ricotta. Remove from the oven and let cool on a wire rack until you can gently remove the weights and parchment from the shell.

6. Fill a large bowl with ice and water.

7. Meanwhile, put a pot of water on the stove to boil over medium-high heat. With a paring knife, lightly score an X on the bottom of each peach and plunge the peaches into the boiling water for about 2 minutes. Using a slotted spoon, remove the peaches and plunge immediately into the ice water bath; remove from the ice water and slip off the skins. Halve the peeled peaches and remove the pits. Thinly slice the peach halves into 6 to 8 slices per half (for a total of 36 to 48 peach slices from the 3 peaches).

8. In a medium bowl, whisk together the ricotta, crème fraîche, 3 Tbsp of the honey, the egg, egg yolks, vanilla, salt, and lemon zest until thoroughly combined. Pour the ricotta mixture in an even layer in the tart shell. Carefully shingle the peaches (that is, arrange them in overlapping concentric circles) on top of the ricotta, doubling up layers if needed. In a small bowl, whisk together the remaining 1 Tbsp honey and the water. Using a pastry brush, lightly brush the tops of the peaches with the mixture.

9. Bake the tart for 50 to 60 minutes, or until the ricotta just sets and the peaches are soft. Remove from the oven and let cool to room temperature on a wire rack. Refrigerate until chilled, 1 to 2 hours. Serve cold. The tart can be stored, well wrapped with plastic wrap, in the refrigerator for up to 2 days.

FLUFFY LEMON FROSTING

- 225 g/8 oz cream cheese, at room temperature
- 85 g/6 Tbsp unsalted butter, very soft
- 1 Tbsp finely grated lemon zest
- 115 g/⅓ cup honey
- 2 tsp vanilla extract
- ⅛ tsp kosher salt

- 130 g/½ cup whole-milk ricotta cheese
- 100 g/½ cup vegetable oil, such as canola
- 225 g/⅔ cup honey
- 1 Tbsp vanilla extract
- 2 Tbsp finely grated lemon zest
- 2 large eggs plus 1 egg yolk
- 180 g/¾ cup crème fraîche (see page 24)
- 280 g/2 cups all-purpose flour
- 2 tsp baking powder
- ¼ tsp baking soda
- ½ tsp kosher salt
- 1 Tbsp finely grated lemon zest

LEMON RICOTTA CUPCAKES
WITH FLUFFY LEMON FROSTING

Flour isn't a restaurant, but we are incredibly lucky to have chefs who would fit in seamlessly in a top restaurant kitchen. To celebrate their talents, we decided to host pop-up charity dinners at each of our locations. Each chef has a chance to show off a little, and we get a chance to give back a little to the communities that have embraced us so fully. Each dinner has its own theme, and each chef selects the nonprofit that is to be the recipient of the dinner proceeds. It's completely win-win!

One aspect of the dinner that remains constant is our dedication to our motto, "Make life sweeter, eat dessert first!" We start off each dinner with a little amuse-bouche (a welcome treat), and it's always something sweet. For the very first pop-up dinner we hosted, I was in the middle of testing recipes for this book, and I knew I wanted to do a little showing off myself. The inaugural guests of this dinner were thus treated to a mini lemon cupcake with a creamy lemon frosting. Would our guests guess that these cakes had no sugar in them? We didn't share that with them until the end, and the reaction was staggering. Some people literally wouldn't take "no sugar" as an answer. It was truly gratifying, and I loved knowing that people were as excited about baking with less sugar as I was. Or at least they were excited about eating the results!

Continued

MAKES

12

CUPCAKES

1. At least 4 hours in advance, make the frosting: Using a stand mixer fitted with the paddle attachment (or with an electric hand mixer), beat the cream cheese on medium speed for at least 3 to 4 minutes, or until perfectly smooth. (Cream cheese has a tendency to lump up easily, so don't skip this step.) Using a rubber spatula, scrape the bowl and add the butter and 1 Tbsp lemon zest. Add the honey, vanilla, and salt and beat well on medium speed until thoroughly combined. Refrigerate the frosting for at least 4 hours before using to firm it up. The frosting can be stored in a covered container in the refrigerator for up to 1 week.

2. Place a rack in the center of the oven and pre-heat to 350°F [175°C]. Butter and flour a standard 12-cup muffin tin, spray with nonstick cooking spray, or line with paper liners.

3. In a medium bowl, whisk together the ricotta, oil, honey, vanilla, and lemon zest until well mixed. Whisk in the eggs and egg yolk until well combined. Whisk in the crème fraîche. In a separate medium bowl, stir together the flour, baking powder, baking soda, and salt. Using a rubber spatula, gently fold the dry ingredients into the wet ingredients until the batter is homogenous. Be careful not to over-mix.

4. Divide the batter evenly among the prepared cups of the muffin tin. Bake for 20 to 25 minutes, or until the cupcakes are pale golden brown and spring back when you press them in the center with your finger. Remove from the oven and let cool completely in the pan on a wire rack.

5. Don't attempt to frost the cupcakes while the least bit warm, or the frosting will slide off. Remove the frosting from the refrigerator and, using an offset spatula or a piping bag, spread or pipe the cupcakes with frosting, garnish with the remaining lemon zest, and serve. The frosted cupcakes can be stored in an airtight container in the refrigerator for up to 3 days. Remove at least 1 hour before serving so the cupcakes are not cold. Garnish with the remaining lemon zest.

HONEY-ALMOND SNACK CAKE

- 100 g/½ cup vegetable oil, such as canola
- 225 g/⅔ cup honey
- 2 tsp vanilla extract
- 2 tsp almond extract
- 2 large eggs plus 2 egg yolks
- 240 g/1 cup crème fraîche (see page 24)
- 210 g/1½ cups all-purpose flour
- 100 g/1 cup almond flour
- 2 tsp baking powder
- ¼ tsp baking soda
- ½ tsp kosher salt

CREAMY FROSTING

- 225 g/8 oz cream cheese, at room temperature
- 85 g/6 Tbsp unsalted butter, very soft
- 115 g/⅓ cup honey
- 2 tsp vanilla extract
- 1 tsp almond extract
- ¼ tsp kosher salt

When I was a kid, I daydreamed that I'd come home from school and, magically, my mom would turn into one of those mothers who would be lavishly frosting a cake for me and my brother to snack on while we did our homework. Instead, there was usually a plate of diced melon, sliced apples, and peeled oranges. Now that I know what goes into most cakes—loads of sugar and, if it's from a box, likely a number of preservatives as well—I understand better why she refused to listen to my wishes. (Mom was magical in other ways.)

Here is a cake that you can feel really great about making for your family. It's sweetened with honey, has a velvety tender crumb, and the frosting is just sweet enough without being over-the-top. You feel good after eating it. Almost as good as if you had eaten a plate of fruit.

(For a terrific gluten-free alternative for this cake, instead of 210 g/ 1½ cups all-purpose flour, try substituting 65 g/½ cup sorghum flour, plus 100 g/½ cup sweet rice flour, plus 85 g/½ cup potato starch. Thanks to Laura, who tried this version and deemed it the best gluten-free cake she's ever tasted!)

1. Place a rack in the center of the oven and preheat to 350°F [175°C]. Butter and flour the bottom and sides of a 9-by-13-in [23-by-33-cm] baking pan, spray with nonstick cooking spray, or butter and line the bottom of the pan with parchment paper.

Continued

MAKES

ONE

9-BY-13-IN
[23-BY-33-CM] CAKE

2. In a medium bowl, whisk together the vegetable oil, honey, vanilla, and almond extract until well mixed. Whisk in the eggs and egg yolks until well combined. Whisk in the crème fraîche. In a separate medium bowl, stir together the all-purpose flour, almond flour, baking powder, baking soda, and salt. Using a rubber spatula, gently fold the dry ingredients into the wet ingredients until thoroughly combined. Scrape the batter into the prepared pan.

3. Bake for 30 to 40 minutes, or until the cake springs back when you poke it in the center and is pale golden brown. Remove from the oven and let cool completely in the pan on a wire rack.

4. Meanwhile, make the frosting: Using a stand mixer fitted with the paddle attachment (or with an electric hand mixer), beat the cream cheese on medium speed for at least 4 minutes, or until perfectly smooth. (Cream cheese has a tendency to lump up easily, so don't skip this step.) Using a rubber spatula, scrape the bowl and add the butter. Add the honey, vanilla, almond extract, and salt and beat well on medium speed until thoroughly combined. The frosting can be stored in a covered container in the refrigerator for up to 1 week.

5. When the cake is completely cool, using a rubber spatula or an offset spatula, frost with creamy frosting and serve. The frosted cake can be stored, well wrapped with plastic wrap or in an airtight container in the refrigerator, for up to 3 days; remove at least 1 hour before serving so the cake is not cold.

CHAPTER FOUR

BAKING WITH MAPLE SYRUP AND MOLASSES

Maple syrup and molasses are the only sweeteners in these recipes. These are unprocessed sugars that have not been stripped of any of their naturally occurring antioxidants and valuable minerals. Maple syrup is high in manganese and zinc; molasses is rich in magnesium, iron, copper, manganese, and potassium. The lists of nutrients in both read a little bit like a vitamin pill. Besides offering health benefits, these two sweeteners are also very versatile in baking. They do more than add just sweetness to a dessert; they also add their unique aromas and fantastic flavors. Maple syrup and molasses work well together, so I've joined them in a few recipes.

- 5 slices thick-cut, applewood-smoked bacon
- 385 g/2¾ cups all-purpose flour
- 2 tsp baking powder
- ½ tsp baking soda
- ½ tsp kosher salt
- 115 g/½ cup cold unsalted butter, cut into 8 to 10 pieces
- 110 g/4 oz Cheddar cheese, cut into ¼-in [6-mm] dice
- 180 g/¾ cup crème fraîche (see page 24)
- 210 g/⅔ cup grade B maple syrup
- 2 large eggs
- 1 Tbsp cornstarch

MAPLE-BACON-CHEDDAR BISCUITS

When I decided to do a low-sugar/no-sugar book, I pondered which sweeteners I would work with instead. Artificial sweeteners were definitely out, but that still left a host of other possibilities for me to play with. Maple syrup is a favorite of mine; I grew up in Texas and had only tried Aunt Jemima pancake syrup (that is, corn syrup and artificial maple flavoring) for breakfast on the rare pancake-breakfast day. Not until I moved up to the Northeast did I have my first taste of true maple syrup: deep, mellow, rich, and buttery. Ever since then I've been hooked. The first *Flour* cookbook features an incredible oatmeal-maple scone and I didn't want to repeat recipes, so my agent immediately suggested, "What about maple-bacon?" I'm not really one for mixing sweet and savory, but here it definitely works. Stacey, this recipe is for you: maple and bacon and Cheddar, all wrapped up in one warm, sweet, addictive treat.

1. Place a rack in the center of the oven and preheat to 300°F [150°C]. Line a baking sheet with parchment paper or aluminum foil.

2. Lay the bacon on the prepared baking sheet, and bake for 25 to 28 minutes, or until about half of each strip is crispy and half is still a little bendy. Remove from the oven and let cool on the baking sheet on a wire rack. When the bacon is cool enough to handle, chop it into ½-in [1-cm] pieces and set aside.

3. Increase the oven temperature to 350°F [175°C].

Continued

MAKES

8

BISCUITS

4. Using a stand mixer fitted with the paddle attachment (or with an electric hand mixer), briefly mix the flour, baking powder, baking soda, and salt on low speed until combined. Add the butter and beat on low speed for 30 seconds to 1 minute, or until the butter is somewhat broken down but there are still pieces about the size of a grape. (Alternatively, use a pastry cutter or two knives to cut the butter into the dry ingredients; proceed as directed.) Add the bacon and Cheddar and beat on low speed for 5 to 10 seconds, or until somewhat mixed into the dry ingredients. (If mixing by hand, use a wooden spoon to mix the bacon and Cheddar into the dough.)

5. In a medium bowl, whisk together the crème fraîche, 105 g/⅓ cup of the maple syrup, and the eggs until thoroughly mixed. With the mixer running on low speed, pour the crème fraîche mixture into the flour-butter mixture and beat for 20 to 30 seconds, or until the dough just comes together. There will probably still be a little loose flour mixture at the bottom of the bowl.

6. Remove the bowl from the mixer. Gather and lift the dough with your hands and turn it over in the bowl so that it starts to pick up the loose flour at the bottom. Turn the dough over several times until all the loose flour is mixed in.

7. Dump the dough onto a well-floured work surface and roll into a rectangle about 6 by 10 in [15 by 25 cm]. With a knife or bench scraper, halve the dough lengthwise and cut each half into 4 pieces to make 8 rectangular biscuits in total. Place the biscuits on the prepared baking sheet. (At this point the unbaked biscuits can be stored in the freezer, tightly wrapped in plastic wrap, for up to one week. If baking directly from the freezer, add 5 to 10 minutes to the baking time and proceed as directed.)

8. Bake for 30 to 35 minutes, or until the biscuits are golden brown. Remove the biscuits from oven and let cool on the baking sheet on a wire rack. In a small saucepan, whisk together the remaining 105 g/⅓ cup maple syrup and the cornstarch and bring to a boil. Remove from the heat. Let the glaze cool and brush onto the room-temperature biscuits.

9. The biscuits are best enjoyed the same day you bake them, but they can be stored in an airtight container at room temperature for up to 3 days. If you keep them for longer than 1 day, refresh them in a 300°F [150°C] oven for 4 to 5 minutes. Or store in the freezer, tightly wrapped in plastic wrap, for up to 1 week; reheat from frozen in a 300°F [150°C] oven for 8 to 10 minutes.

MOLASSES GINGERBREAD

- 225 g/1 cup unsalted butter, melted and cooled
- 1 Tbsp finely grated orange zest
- 2 Tbsp peeled and grated fresh ginger
- 80 g/¼ cup grade B maple syrup
- 1 large egg plus 2 egg yolks
- 385 g/2¾ cups all-purpose flour
- 1 Tbsp baking powder
- 4 tsp ground ginger
- 2 tsp ground cinnamon
- ½ tsp ground cloves
- ½ tsp freshly ground pepper
- 1 tsp kosher salt
- 240 g/¾ cup mild unsulphured molasses (not blackstrap)
- 120 g/½ cup boiling water
- ½ tsp baking soda

Spicy and dark, this gingerbread is a cinch to put together once you gather all of the spices. Don't skimp on any of them—they all come together to make a rich, fragrant cake that keeps well and gets more flavorful as it sits—though I don't think you'll have a chance to find out, as this treat goes quick once it comes out of the oven. It tastes a little like gingerbread men in cake form. It makes for a pretty wonderful breakfast as well, lightly toasted and slathered with soft butter.

1. Place a rack in the center of the oven and preheat to 350°F [175°C]. Butter and flour an 8-in [20-cm] round cake pan.

2. In a large bowl, vigorously whisk together the butter, orange zest, fresh ginger, and maple syrup until combined. Add the egg and egg yolks and whisk well until the mixture is homogenous.

3. In a medium bowl, using a wooden spoon, stir together the flour, baking powder, ground ginger, cinnamon, cloves, pepper, and salt. In a separate bowl, whisk together the molasses, boiling water, and baking soda. It will foam up! Add about one-third of the dry ingredients to the butter mixture and, with a whisk using a folding motion, fold until incorporated. Immediately pour about half of the molasses mixture into the bowl and fold until the mixture is combined. Add another one-third of the dry ingredients and mix until incorporated. Add the rest of the molasses mixture and mix until incorporated. Add the remaining dry ingredients and fold until the batter is fully combined.

4. Scrape the batter into the prepared pan. Bake for 35 to 45 minutes, or until the top of the cake is firm and springs back when you press it lightly in the center. Remove the cake from the oven and let cool in the pan on a wire rack. The cake can be stored in an airtight container at room temperature for up to 3 days.

MAKES

ONE

8-IN [20-CM] CAKE

- 150 g/1½ cups fresh or frozen cranberries, chopped
- 160 g/½ cup grade B maple syrup
- 115 g/½ cup unsalted butter, at room temperature
- 2 large eggs
- 245 g/1¾ cups all-purpose flour
- 50 g/½ cup medium-coarse cornmeal
- 1½ tsp baking powder
- ¼ tsp baking soda
- ½ tsp kosher salt
- 120 g/½ cup buttermilk
- 2 tsp vanilla extract

CRANBERRY-CORNMEAL-MAPLE BREAD

As crazy as it sounds, when people ask me, "What's your favorite recipe out of your cookbooks?" I feel like I'm being disloyal to the other recipes if I choose any one in particular. (As if the recipes had feelings!) It's really hard to pick just one favorite when you've worked so hard on each one, getting it just right to share with the world. That said, I am extremely fond of the Maple-Cranberry-Pecan Breakfast Cake from the first *Flour* book. While I won't say it's my favorite recipe, I will say that pancakes are my favorite breakfast indulgence, and this breakfast cake tastes exactly like pancakes. Here, I've created a less-sweet version that truly tastes just as good if not better than its inspiration. By using sweet crunchy cornmeal and cooking the cranberries in a little maple syrup before mixing into the batter, you get a rich, fragrant quick bread that makes for an excellent breakfast.

1. Place a rack in the center of the oven and preheat to 350°F [175°C]. Butter and flour a 9-by-5-in [23-by-13-cm] loaf pan, or butter and line the bottom and sides with parchment paper.

2. Put the cranberries and maple syrup in a small saucepan and cook gently over medium heat for 2 to 3 minutes, or until the cranberries soften and warm up in the maple syrup. Remove from the heat and set aside.

MAKES

ONE
9-IN [23-CM] LOAF

3. Using a stand mixer fitted with the paddle attachment (or with an electric hand mixer), beat the butter on medium speed for 1 to 2 minutes, or until softened and light. (If using a hand mixer, beat for a few minutes longer.) Drain the maple syrup from the cranberries and slowly add the warm syrup to the butter, continuing to beat on low speed until the syrup is completely mixed in. Scrape the bowl and the beater with a rubber spatula to ensure that the butter and syrup mix together well. Add the eggs and beat for 2 to 3 minutes, or until the eggs are mixed in.

4. In a small bowl, combine the flour, cornmeal, baking powder, baking soda, and salt. Stir to mix well. Add about half of the flour mixture to the butter-egg mixture and, using a rubber spatula, fold by hand to combine. Add the buttermilk and vanilla and continue to fold. Add the remaining flour mixture and fold until all of the ingredients are well blended. Fold in the reserved cranberries.

5. Pour the batter into the prepared pan. Bake for 60 to 70 minutes, or until the quick bread springs back when you press it in the center with your finger. Due to the lack of sugar, which contributes to browning, the quick bread won't get very golden brown; it will color a little on top, but use touch to determine when it is ready to remove from the oven. Remove from the oven and let cool on a wire rack. When cool, invert to pop the quick bread out of the pan.

6. The quick bread can be stored, well wrapped with plastic wrap, at room temperature for up to 4 days. It's terrific served toasted or just as is. (I love it slathered with a little extra butter.)

- 170 g/¾ cup unsalted butter, melted and cooled
- 160 g/½ cup mild unsulphured molasses (not blackstrap)
- 80 g/¼ cup grade B maple syrup
- 1 Tbsp vanilla extract
- 3 large eggs
- 120 g/½ cup apple juice
- 420 g/15 oz pumpkin purée
- 420 g/3 cups all-purpose flour
- 2 tsp baking powder
- ½ tsp baking soda
- 1 tsp kosher salt
- 4 tsp ground ginger
- 4 tsp ground cinnamon
- ½ tsp freshly grated nutmeg
- ⅛ tsp ground cloves
- 1 medium Empire, McIntosh, Golden Delicious, Gala, or other sweet baking apple, peeled, cored, and diced small

MAKES

12

MUFFINS

PUMPKIN-APPLE SPICE MUFFINS

Spices can be polarizing! It turns out whenever you make something with a lot of different spices, you'll end up with a lot of different opinions about whether or not there are too many spices or not enough. I felt like Goldilocks when making these muffins over and over to get the spices "just right." I knew we finally got it down when Keith, one of my testers, made these for a brunch with a group of Flour bakers and they unanimously gave a thumbs-up. That's one heck of a group of tough critics to impress. The apple juice and chopped apples add a lovely sweetness and help make the muffins super moist.

1. Place a rack in the center of the oven and preheat to 350°F [175°C]. Butter and flour a standard 12-cup muffin tin, spray with nonstick cooking spray, or line with paper liners.

2. Using a stand mixer fitted with the paddle attachment (or with an electric hand mixer or by hand with a whisk), beat the butter, molasses, maple syrup, and vanilla on medium speed for 1 to 2 minutes, or until combined.

3. With the mixer on low speed, add the eggs, one at a time, beating for about 30 seconds after each addition to combine the eggs and butter-molasses mixture thoroughly. Scrape the bottom and sides of the bowl with a rubber spatula. With the mixer on low speed, add the apple juice and pumpkin purée and beat for about 30 seconds, or until combined. The mixture will look somewhat curdled—don't worry, it will all come together once you mix in the flour.

4. In a separate large bowl, with a wooden spoon, stir together the flour, baking powder, baking soda, salt, ginger, cinnamon, nutmeg, cloves, and apple. Dump the butter-egg mixture into the dry ingredients and fold carefully with a rubber spatula or a wooden spoon just until all of the dry and wet ingredients are well combined.

5. Using a small ice cream scoop or a large spoon, scoop the muffin batter into the prepared tins. Fill the cups all the way to the top and overflowing. It will seem like too much batter for 12 muffins, but the batter does not spread that much so you can overfill the cups.

6. Bake for 35 to 45 minutes, or until the muffins spring back lightly when you press them in the center and a toothpick comes out clean when you insert in the center of a muffin. This is a very heavy and moist batter, so don't under-bake or they will come out gummy. Let the muffins cool in the pan on a wire rack for 20 minutes and then carefully remove them from the pan.

7. The muffins can be stored at room temperature in an airtight container for up to 3 days. Or store them in the freezer, tightly wrapped in plastic wrap, for up to 3 weeks; thaw them overnight on the counter. The unbaked muffin batter can be stored in an airtight container in the refrigerator for up to 2 days.

- 170 g/¾ cup unsalted butter, melted and cooled
- 240 g/¾ cup mild unsulphured molasses (not blackstrap)
- 80 g/¼ cup grade B maple syrup
- 1 large egg
- 210 g/1½ cups all-purpose flour
- 4 tsp ground ginger
- 2 tsp ground cinnamon
- ½ tsp ground cloves
- ½ tsp freshly ground pepper
- 1 tsp kosher salt

KEITH'S
SUPER-SNAPPY GINGERSNAPS

Our ginger-molasses cookies are rightfully beloved among Flour customers: the cookies are thick, chewy, spicy, buttery, and redolent with ginger. I adore them. In trying to come up with a version made without sugar, I knew that the flavor profile would work well by substituting molasses for all of the sugar. And because molasses has such a strong flavor, I also knew I could get by with less.

It turns out that *just* molasses in this cookie was a bit too distinctive. The cookie needed sweetness from the molasses, but the flavor was so sharp I had to cut down on the molasses and add a bit of mellower maple syrup. Once I got the sweetness level spot on (typically this recipe uses 400 g/2 cups of sugar), the next challenge was the texture. I wanted something different from our ginger-molasses cookie—something crispy and crunchy. But without sugar, which helps makes pastries crunchy and caramelized, I found it really challenging to get that snap I was looking for. Keith to the rescue! Keith was a cookbook tester for me for the second Flour book, *Flour, Too*, and subsequently he became a baker with us at Flour. He took this on as a personal challenge to make a crispy gingersnap, and he tested and retested various versions until he came up with this one. (The incentive that I would name the cookie after him didn't hurt, either!) So here you have it—Keith's cookies, which are named after him not only because of his work on these but also because of his super-bright, snappy nature! Note that there is a fair amount of waiting time in making these—waiting for the dough to chill and waiting for the cookies to cool and crisp in the oven.

Continued

MAKES ABOUT
24
COOKIES

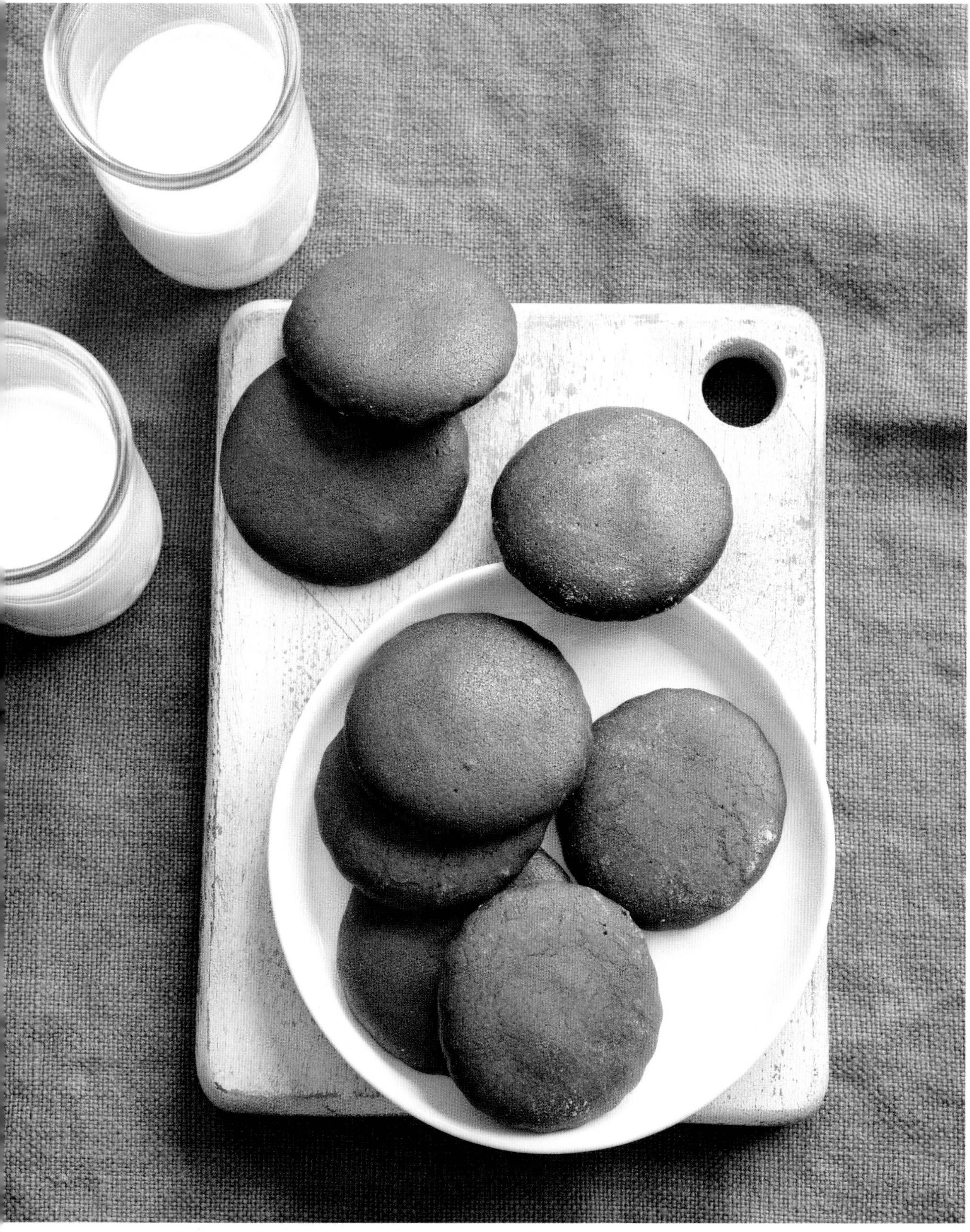

1. In a medium bowl, vigorously whisk together the molasses, and maple syrup until well combined. Add the egg and whisk again, making sure all the ingredients are well mixed.

2. In a small bowl, with a wooden spoon, combine the flour, ginger, cinnamon, cloves, pepper, and salt, and stir to evenly distribute the spices. Add the dry ingredients to the wet ingredients and stir well with a wooden spoon until well mixed. The dough will be soft.

3. Refrigerate the dough for 1 to 2 hours, or until it stiffens up. It is really sticky, so it needs to chill before you can roll it out. Remove from the refrigerator and roll it between two pieces of parchment paper into a 10-in [25-cm] square about ¼ in [6 mm] thick. Place the dough on a baking sheet and freeze for at least 3 hours or up to overnight.

4. Place racks in the center and top shelves of the oven and preheat to 350°F [175°C]. Line two baking sheets with parchment paper.

5. Remove the dough from the freezer and carefully peel off the parchment paper from one side of the dough. Lightly flour the dough, lay the parchment paper back on the dough, and flip it over. Carefully peel off the second piece of parchment paper and lightly flour the dough. Using a 2-in [5-cm] round cutter, dipping into flour each time to prevent sticking, cut out circles of dough and place on the prepared baking sheets, 12 cookies to a sheet. These spread a fair amount, so space them about 2 in [5 cm] apart. Reroll scraps of dough, reflour the dough, and continue to cut out cookies, working quickly to prevent the dough from softening too much. You should get about 24 cookies.

6. Because these cookies don't contain any granulated sugar to help make them crispy, they get their snap by first being baked until they are firm in the oven and then drying out for several hours after you turn off the oven until they become crunchy. You can bake both baking sheets at once or bake them one after the other; if you bake both at once, use the top and center racks of your oven and switch the rack position about halfway through baking (that is, the top sheet moves to the middle rack and middle sheet moves to the top rack).

7. Bake the cookies for 14 to 16 minutes, rotating the cookie sheet about 8 minutes in to ensure even baking, or until the cookies are firm to the touch and baked through. Turn off the oven and let the cookies crisp up in the oven until the oven completely cools, ideally overnight. The gingersnaps will slowly dry out and get crispy as they cool. Remove from the oven and eat your snappy snaps! The cookies can be stored in an airtight container at room temperature for up to 1 week.

STICKY TOFFEE PUDDING
WITH MAPLE SAUCE

- 240 g/1 cup pitted and chopped Medjool dates
- 120 g/½ cup hot water
- ½ tsp baking soda
- 175 g/1¼ cups all-purpose flour
- 1 tsp baking powder
- ½ tsp kosher salt
- 2 tsp vanilla extract
- 3 Tbsp grade B maple syrup
- 55 g/4 Tbsp unsalted butter, melted and cooled
- 2 large eggs

MAPLE SAUCE

- 80 g/¼ cup grade B maple syrup
- 115 g/½ cup unsalted butter, melted and cooled
- 60 g/¼ cup heavy cream, at room temperature or warmed (if it is cold, it could cause the butter to lump when mixed)

We make an incredible sticky toffee pudding at Myers+Chang that we heap with whipped cream and douse with warm maple sauce to order. It's super sweet with sticky dates and loads of brown sugar and is the perfect dessert to eat in the snowy, cold winter months. Here, I've taken out the sugar and added maple syrup instead, and I've also tamed the sweetness so you can really taste the deep, fruity flavors of the dates. This cake is moist and full of flavor, and you'd never guess there was no sugar. You'll adore the sauce and end up putting it on everything—it goes great on pancakes and ice cream, too. The name "pudding" is deceptive if you haven't had this dessert before; it hails from England where they often call steamed cakes "pudding."

1. Place a rack in the center of the oven and preheat to 350°F [175°C]. Butter and flour an 8-in [20-cm] round cake pan, or butter and line the bottom with parchment paper.

2. Put the dates in a small bowl and add the hot water. Add the baking soda and stir to dissolve; the baking soda will soften the skins of the dates. Let sit for 10 to 15 minutes.

3. With a food processor or a blender, combine the dates and soaking water and process until smooth. Add the flour, baking powder, salt, vanilla, and maple syrup and process until well mixed. Add the butter and eggs and process until well mixed.

4. Pour the batter into the prepared pan. Bake for 35 to 45 minutes, or until the cake is golden brown and springs back when you press it in the center. Remove from the oven and let cool in the pan on a wire rack.

Continued

MAKES

ONE
8-IN [20-CM] CAKE

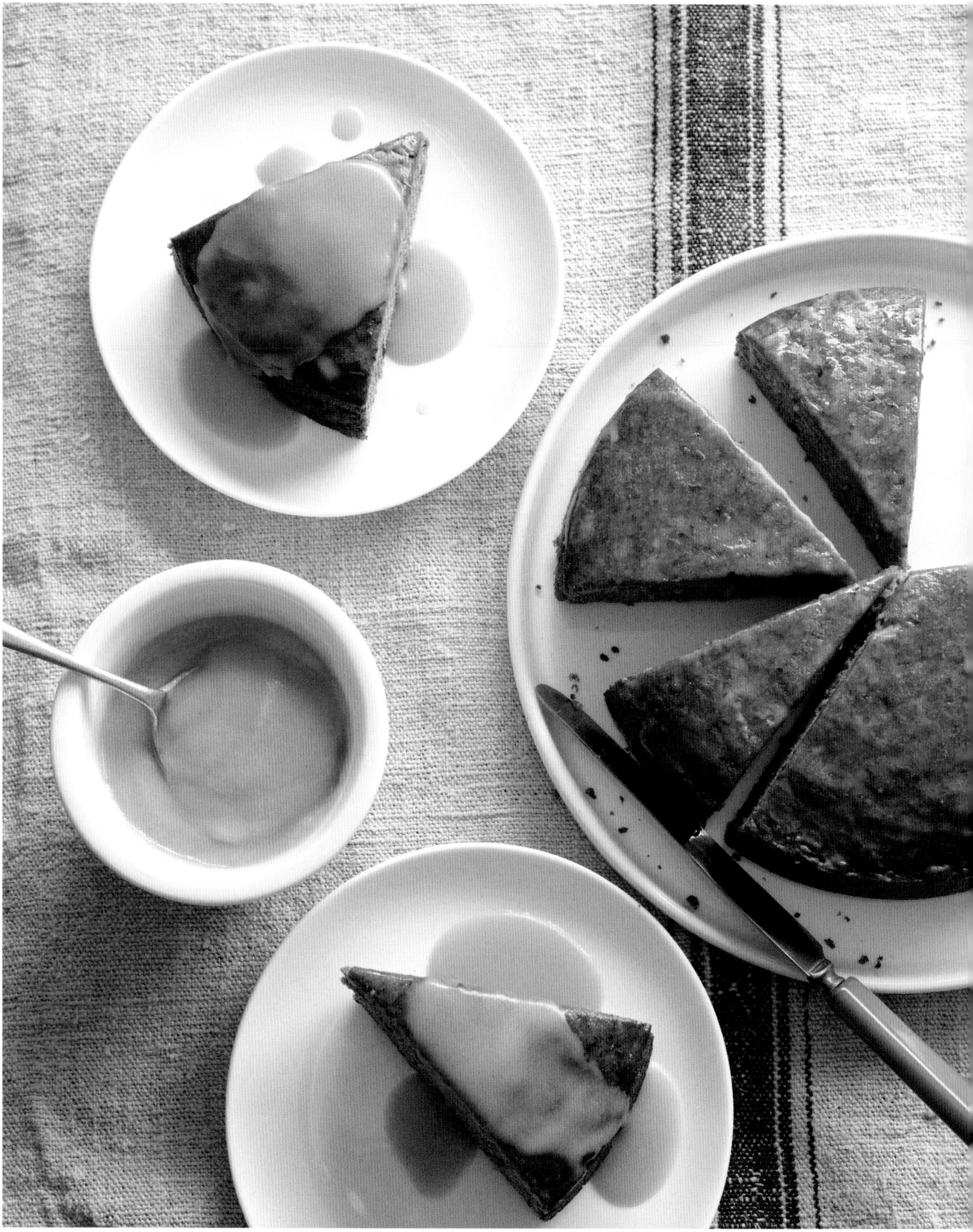

5. Meanwhile, make the sauce: In a medium bowl, whisk together the maple syrup and butter until blended. Slowly whisk in the cream. The mixture should be somewhat soupy. Let the sauce sit at room temperature as the cake bakes.

6. Line a plate with parchment paper. When the cake is out of the oven, pour about one-third of the sauce evenly over the top of the cake while it cools. When the cake is completely cool, invert it onto the lined plate and then quickly invert it again onto a serving plate so that it is right-side up. Serve slices of the cake warm or at room temperature with extra sauce generously ladled on top. The cake can be stored, well wrapped in plastic wrap, at room temperature for up to 3 days. The sauce can be stored in an airtight container in the refrigerator for up to 1 week; warm it in a small saucepan over medium-low heat before serving.

- 960 g/4 cups whole milk
- 100 g/½ cup medium-coarse yellow or white cornmeal
- 55 g/4 Tbsp unsalted butter
- 215 g/⅔ cup mild unsulphured molasses (not blackstrap)
- 1 Tbsp vanilla extract
- ¾ tsp kosher salt
- ½ tsp ground ginger
- ½ tsp ground cinnamon
- 2 large eggs
- Unsweetened heavy cream, whipped to soft peaks, for garnish

OLD-FASHIONED INDIAN PUDDING

If you're not a native New Englander, you may have never had Indian pudding before or even heard of it. I grew up in Texas, so my introduction to this creamy, mellow dessert wasn't until I had been in Boston for quite some time and was learning to bake at my first pastry job. Rick Katz, my pastry chef at Bentonwood Bakery, offered it at the holidays and after my first taste, it became one of my favorite desserts that I learned to make from Rick.

I'm on a mission to bring it back with this recipe. Many people are quite nostalgic for this pudding, especially if they grew up in the Northeast. It has a lovely smooth texture similar to flan with a bit more heft from the cornmeal. It is easy to make, smells incredible as it's baking, and the flavor is terrific—not too sweet, rich, comforting. People are always excited to eat this, and it is a huge hit with friends and family.

1. Place a rack in the center of the oven and preheat to 250°F [120°C]. Butter a 9-by-13-in [23-by-33-cm] baking pan or a 9-in [23-cm] round cake pan.

2. Bring 840 g/3½ cups of the milk just to a boil in a large saucepan over medium-high heat. Slowly pour in the cornmeal while whisking constantly. Decrease the heat to medium and cook, whisking constantly, for 10 to 12 minutes, or until the mixture is very thick. Remove from the heat, whisk in the butter, and set aside.

3. In a small bowl, whisk together the molasses, vanilla, salt, ginger, cinnamon, and eggs. Pour the molasses mixture into the cornmeal mixture while whisking constantly. Scrape into the prepared pan and carefully pour the remaining 120 g/½ cup milk on top in a spiral pattern. The milk will slowly sink to the bottom.

SERVES

10 TO 12

4. Bake for 2 hours, or until the top of the custard is barely set and when you press it in the center with your finger, it no longer feels liquid underneath. Remove from the oven and let cool on a wire rack.

5. Using a stand mixer fitted with the whisk attachment (or with an electric hand mixer or by hand with a whisk), whip the cream on medium speed until it holds soft peaks that droop a little when the whisk is lifted. Serve the pudding at room temperature or chilled with whipped cream as garnish. The pudding can be stored, well wrapped with plastic wrap, in the refrigerator for up to 4 days.

- 480 g/1½ cups grade B maple syrup
- 480 g/2 cups heavy cream
- 240 g/1 cup whole milk
- 4 large eggs plus 1 egg yolk
- ¼ tsp kosher salt
- ¼ tsp vanilla extract

MAPLE CRÈME CARAMEL

I adore simple custards. The fewer ingredients, the better. This crème caramel is a step up from plain standard vanilla in that it uses maple syrup both as the caramel for the sauce and to sweeten the custard itself. Each serving has three tablespoons of maple syrup, which is not a small amount, but the reward is a truly sensational and deeply flavored dessert made without any white sugar.

1. Place 320 g/1 cup of the maple syrup in a medium or large saucepan and bring to a boil over medium-high heat. Decrease the heat to medium-low and simmer for 30 to 40 minutes, or until thickened, dark, and reduced to about ½ cup [120 ml]. (It foams up in the pan, so be sure to use a large enough pan so it doesn't boil over. Once it foams, turn down the heat so it simply simmers—if it keeps foaming, it will start to burn. Watch it carefully!)

2. Place a rack in the center of the oven and preheat to 350°F [175°C].

3. Place eight 4-oz [120-ml] ramekins in a roasting pan with high sides and carefully pour the reduced maple syrup into the bottom of the ramekins, about 1 Tbsp in each one.

4. In a large bowl, whisk together the remaining 160 g/½ cup maple syrup, the cream, milk, eggs, egg yolk, salt, and vanilla until thoroughly combined. Pour the custard into the ramekins, filling each evenly. Carefully carry the roasting pan with the ramekins to the oven and place on the middle rack. Pour hot water into the roasting pan so it comes at least halfway up the sides of the ramekins. (This is a water bath and will protect your custards from over-baking.)

MAKES

8

CUSTARDS

5. Bake for 40 to 50 minutes, or until the custards jiggle very slowly like Jell-O when you wiggle them around. Remove the roasting pan from the oven and let the custards cool in the pan until they are cool enough to handle. Store in the refrigerator, covered with plastic wrap, for at least overnight, or up to 4 days before serving.

6. To serve, run a small paring knife around the edge of each ramekin and quickly invert the custard onto a serving plate. Tap the bottom of the ramekin until the custard slides out. The maple syrup will have created a sauce that pours out on top of the custard.

- 480 g/2 cups whole milk
- 480 g/2 cups heavy cream
- 8 egg yolks
- 240 g/¾ cup grade B maple syrup
- 1 Tbsp vanilla extract
- ¼ tsp kosher salt
- 1 recipe Maple Pecans (recipe follows)

MAPLE PECAN ICE CREAM

Growing up in Texas, I only read about snow. We certainly didn't see it during our mild winters in Houston. When I was around eight, we moved temporarily to Denver for one year for my dad's job. Boy, did I get introduced to snow! I'd read about making maple snow—drizzling fresh snow with maple syrup and eating it by the bowlful—so the very first snowfall, that's exactly what I did. I made maple snow for the whole family, even our dog. It's one of my earliest memories of trying to follow a recipe.

Ever since, I've had a soft spot for frozen maple-y treats. This ice cream is many steps up from simple maple snow and is one of my favorite winter desserts. I often make a double batch of nuts when making this recipe, once for the ice cream and once for snacking.

1. Set a fine-mesh strainer over a large container.

2. In a medium saucepan, combine the milk and cream and heat over medium-high heat until it is scalded—that is, small bubbles form on the edges of the mixture and it almost, but not quite, comes to a boil. Put the egg yolks in a medium bowl and slowly whisk in the maple syrup until well combined. Slowly ladle a little of the hot cream into the egg-syrup mixture and whisk to combine. Continue slowly adding the hot cream to the yolks, whisking all the while, until all of the cream is mixed in. (Adding the hot liquid slowly is called tempering, which allows you to introduce the hot liquid to the cold egg yolks slowly and gently so that you combine them without scrambling the yolks.)

MAKES ABOUT

1½

QUARTS [1.4 L]

3. Return the whole mixture to the saucepan and cook over medium heat, stirring constantly with a wooden spoon, for 6 to 8 minutes, or until the mixture thickens and coats the back of the spoon. The mixture will seem thin at first, then it will start to steam, and then it will start to develop a little body and get thicker. Remove from the heat and immediately strain the mixture through the fine-mesh strainer into the container. Whisk in the vanilla and salt.

4. Place the ice cream base, covered, in the refrigerator until completely cold, at least 4 hours or up to overnight. Churn in an ice cream maker according to the manufacturer's directions. When the ice cream has finished churning, add in the pecans and mix well with a wooden spoon to evenly distribute the nuts. Transfer the ice cream to a storage container and freeze for at least 3 hours to allow it to ripen. During the ripening process, the ice cream becomes harder and smoother and the flavors develop more fully.

5. Store the ice cream in an airtight container in the freezer for up to 2 weeks.

MAPLE PECANS

MAKES ABOUT 215 G/1½ CUPS

- 150 g/1½ cups pecan pieces
- 80 g/¼ cup grade B maple syrup

1. Place a rack in the center of the oven and preheat to 350°F [175°C]. Put the pecans on a baking sheet and toast for 8 to 10 minutes, or until lightly toasted. Set aside to cool.

2. In a small saucepan, mix together the maple syrup and pecans. With a wooden spoon, stir over medium heat until the syrup is mixed well into the nuts. After 2 to 3 minutes, or when the nuts are completely coated with syrup, the syrup is starting to caramelize on the bottom of the pan, and the bottom of the pan is dry, remove from the heat and pour out onto a plate. Let cool and then chop up before using. The nuts can be stored in an airtight container at room temperature for up to 2 days.

DONUTS

- 2½ tsp/1 pkg active dry yeast, or 18 g/¾ oz fresh cake yeast
- 120 g/½ cup whole milk, at room temperature
- 375 g/2⅔ cups all-purpose flour
- 80 g/¼ cup grade B maple syrup
- 1½ tsp kosher salt
- 2 large eggs
- 75 g/6 Tbsp unsalted butter, at room temperature, cut into 6 to 8 pieces
- 100 g/½ cup maple sugar
- Vegetable oil for frying

MAPLE CREAM FILLING

- 240 g/1 cup heavy cream
- 120 g/6 Tbsp grade B maple syrup

MAPLE CREAM DONUTS

I didn't think our popular donuts could get any better, but these just might have done it. We only make donuts once a week—each one is fried and filled by hand, and they go fast. These donuts are made with maple sugar in addition to maple syrup (you can buy maple sugar from reputable sources online). You roll the warm donuts in the maple sugar, which makes them nice and crunchy on the outside. The filling is simply whipped cream sweetened with a bit of maple syrup. The caramel-y flavor of the maple cream combines with the crunchy, sugary fried dough to make a delectable treat.

1. To make the donuts: Using a stand mixer fitted with the dough hook attachment, combine the yeast and milk. Stir together briefly and let sit for about 1 minute to dissolve the yeast. Add the flour, maple syrup, salt, and eggs and mix on low speed for about 1 minute, or until the dough comes together. Once the dough has developed, mix on low speed for 2 to 3 minutes more. Add the butter, a few pieces at a time, and continue to mix for 5 to 6 minutes, or until the butter is completely mixed in and the dough becomes soft and cohesive. Remove from the bowl and wrap tightly in plastic wrap. Refrigerate for at least 6 hours or up to overnight.

2. Lightly flour a baking sheet. Remove the dough from the refrigerator and roll it out on a well-floured surface into a 9-in [23-cm] square about ½ in [1 cm] thick. Using a 3-in [8-cm] round cutter, cut out donuts and arrange them on the prepared baking sheet. Reroll the scraps and keep cutting until all the dough is used. Cover the donuts with plastic wrap and let sit in a draft-free, warm place (78 to 82°F [25 to 28°C] is ideal; an area near the stove or in the oven with only the pilot light on is good) for 1½ to 2½ hours to proof, until the donuts have about doubled in height and feel poufy and pillowy.

3. Line a baking sheet with paper towels. Place the maple sugar in a small bowl.

Continued

MAKES

DONUTS

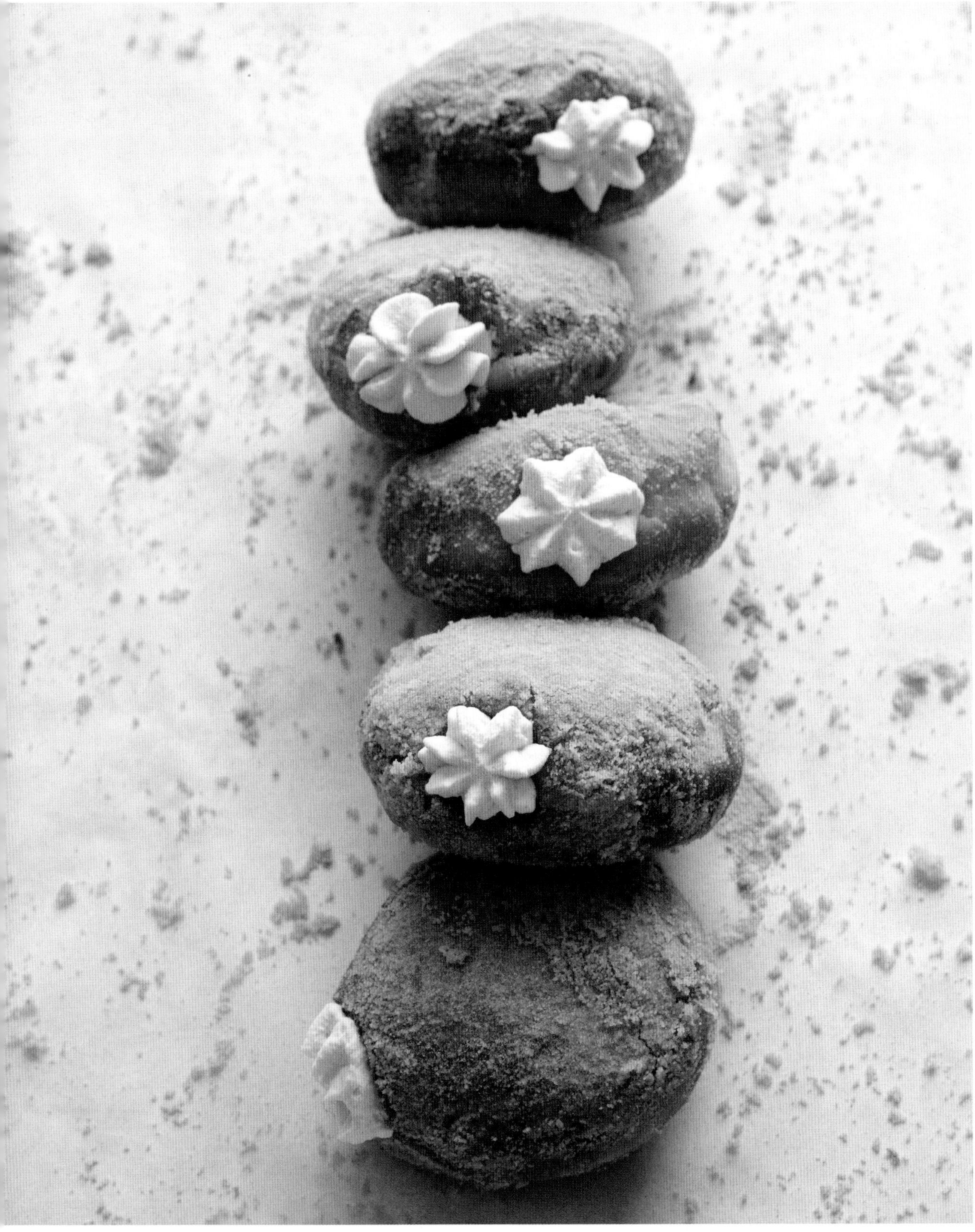

4. When ready to fry, fill a large saucepan with about 3 in [8 cm] of vegetable oil and heat on medium heat. To test the oil, throw in a pinch of flour; when the flour sizzles, the oil is ready. If you have a thermometer, the oil temperature should read 350°F [175°C]. Working in batches, place the donuts in the hot oil, being careful not to crowd them. Let them brown on one side for 2 to 3 minutes and then gently flip them over to brown on the other side, 2 to 3 minutes more. When both sides are completely browned, remove them from the oil with a slotted spoon. Place the donuts on the prepared baking sheet to cool for a few minutes, until cool enough to handle.

5. While the donuts are still warm, toss them one by one in the maple sugar to coat. Return them to the sheet to cool completely, 30 to 40 minutes. When donuts are completely cool, use a paring knife to poke a hole deep into the side of each donut, wiggling the knife around a bit to create a cavity for the cream.

6. To make the filling: Using a stand mixer fitted with the whisk attachment (or with an electric hand mixer or by hand with a whisk), whip the cream on medium speed until stiff peaks form when the beater is lifted and then whip in the maple syrup.

7. When ready to fill the donuts, fill a pastry bag fitted with a small round or star tip with maple cream and pipe 3 to 4 Tbsp filling into each donut. If you don't have a pastry bag, you can fill a heavy-duty plastic bag with the maple cream, cut off one corner to create an opening for the cream, and pipe the cream into the donuts. Serve immediately.

PEAR-MAPLE TARTE TATIN

- 160 g/½ cup grade B maple syrup
- 2 Tbsp unsalted butter
- ½ recipe Quick Puff Pastry (page 164)
- 5 or 6 medium Bosc pears, peeled, halved, and cored
- Crème fraîche (see page 24) or unsweetened whipped cream for garnish

Tarte Tatin is a classic French dessert that purportedly was the happy result of a mistake in the kitchen when a baker made a tart, forgot to line the pie tin with pie crust, and threw it on top instead. It ended up baking into a glorious upside-down tart. It's one of my all-time favorite desserts made with apples, pears, or quince (or all three!). In this version, the sweet Bosc pears bake in a rich syrup that infuses them with the unmistakable flavor of maple. The pears exude a lot of juice while in the oven, so we simmer the whole tart in the pan on the stove after it comes out to reduce and caramelize all of the juices.

1. In a medium saucepan, bring the maple syrup to a boil over medium-high heat. Decrease the heat to medium-low and simmer for 15 to 25 minutes, or until thickened, dark, and reduced to about ¼ cup [60 ml]. (It foams up in the pan, so be sure to use a large enough pan so it doesn't boil over. Once it foams, turn down the heat so it simply simmers—if it keeps foaming it will start to burn. Watch it carefully! It will look like it's boiling away, so keep decreasing the heat to keep it at a low simmer.) Remove from the heat and whisk in the butter. Pour the maple butter into a 9-in [23-cm] round cake pan. It may harden into a firm mass—do your best to spread it evenly on the bottom of the pan, but don't stress about it.

2. On a well-floured work surface, roll the pastry dough into a circle about 10 in [25 cm] diameter and about ¼ in [6 mm] thick. Don't be afraid to be rough with the dough: flip it upside down, turn it side to side, and pound it with the rolling pin to flatten it as you roll it into a nice circle. Place the dough in the refrigerator to rest for at least 20 minutes or up to 1 day.

3. Place a rack in the center of the oven and preheat to 350°F [175°C].

Continued

MAKES

ONE

9-IN [23-CM] TART

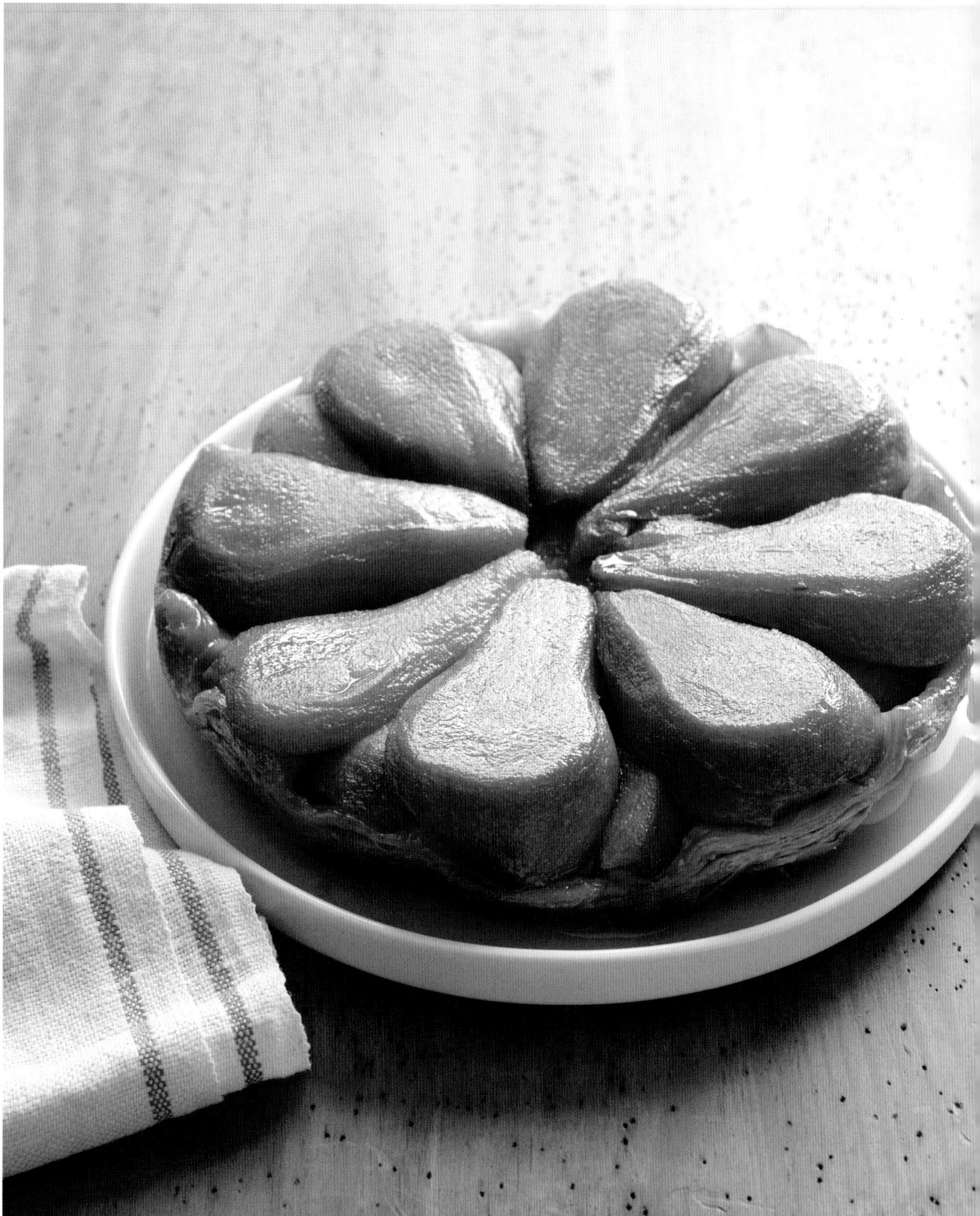

4. Place the pears, rounded-side down, in the caramel in the cake pan, as close together as possible and overlapping them a bit to cover the entire bottom of the pan. You want every single possible bottom surface of the pan to be covered with pears; the fruit cooks down and reduces somewhat in the oven, so don't be shy about packing the fruit in tightly. When you have covered the bottom layer as best as you can, cut any remaining pear halves in quarters or eighths so you can better layer the pears on top of each other, arranging the fruit so that it is fairly level on top.

5. Remove the dough circle from the refrigerator and trim it so that it is an even circle, keeping it about 10 in [25 cm] in diameter. Drape the dough directly on top of the pears and tuck the edges of the dough around the fruit into the sides of the pan. Bake for 70 to 80 minutes, or until the puff pastry is deep golden brown and the juices from the pears are bubbling up along the sides of the pan. Remove from the oven. Heat a burner on the stove to medium-high and carefully place the cake pan directly onto the burner. Bring the extra juice and syrup that has formed from baking the pears to a boil. Watch the juices carefully along the edge of the pan and let them boil for 7 to 10 minutes to thicken them up and caramelize. Place the tart on a wire rack and let cool for 20 to 30 minutes, or until it is cool enough to handle.

6. Place a large serving platter on top of the tart and quickly and carefully invert the pan so the puff pastry circle is on the bottom and the fruit is on top. Rearrange the fruit, if necessary, as sometimes it gets jostled loose and falls off the pastry. Serve warm or at room temperature with crème fraîche or unsweetened whipped cream. The tart can be stored in an airtight container at room temperature for up to 3 days.

- Pâte Brisée (see page 88)
- 420 g/15 oz pumpkin purée
- 1 tsp ground ginger
- 1 tsp ground cinnamon
- ½ tsp freshly grated nutmeg, plus more for garnish
- ⅛ tsp ground cloves
- ½ tsp kosher salt
- 240 g/1 cup heavy cream, plus more, whipped to soft peaks, for garnish
- 2 tsp vanilla extract
- 160 g/½ cup grade B maple syrup
- 3 large eggs

MAPLE-PUMPKIN PIE

Our super-famous pumpkin pie at Flour is refashioned here without any actual sugar and instead uses maple syrup to sweeten the pumpkin. What I love about this version is that without the sugar, you really taste the pumpkin. The mellow maple flavors go especially well with the warm spices, and the pumpkin custard is silky and velvety. You'll serve this to rave reviews.

1. Place a rack in the center of the oven and preheat to 350°F [175°C].

2. Remove the pastry dough from the refrigerator and knead it slightly to make it malleable if it feels stiff. Using a rolling pin, press the dough to flatten it into disk about ½ in [1 cm] thick. Generously flour your work surface and the dough disk. Carefully roll out the disk into a circle about 12 in [30 cm] in diameter. Make sure the table you are rolling on is well floured so that the dough does not stick to it; likewise make sure the disk itself is floured well enough to keep your rolling pin from sticking to it. Roll from the center of the disk outward and gently rotate the disk a quarter turn after each roll to ensure that the disk gets stretched out evenly into a nice circle. Don't worry if the dough breaks a bit, especially towards the edges. You can easily patch these tears up once you've lined your pie plate.

3. Once the dough circle is about 12 in [30 cm] in diameter, roll it gently around the rolling pin and then unfurl it on top of a 9-in [13-cm] aluminum or glass pie plate. Press the dough gently into the bottom and sides of the plate. Either pleat the overhanging dough with your fingers evenly all around for a more dramatic edge, or use scissors to trim the overhang, leaving a ½-in [1-cm] lip around the edge (to allow for shrinkage in the oven). Use any scraps or odd pieces to patch up any tears or missing bits.

Continued

MAKES

ONE
9-IN [23-CM] PIE

4. Refrigerate the pie shell for at least 30 minutes. (The gluten needs a little time to relax so it doesn't shrink as much in the oven). The unbaked pie shell can be stored, tightly wrapped in plastic wrap, in the refrigerator for up to 3 days or in the freezer for up to 4 weeks. If frozen, the pie shell can be baked directly from the freezer.

5. Blind bake (that is, prebake) the shell so it doesn't get soggy when you eventually fill it with pumpkin filling: Line the shell with parchment paper or a large coffee filter and then fill it with pie weights, uncooked beans, uncooked rice, or even well-washed marble-size rocks. Press down slightly on the weights to make sure the shell is entirely filled and place in the oven. Bake for 35 to 40 minutes, or until the shell is brown on the edges and pale and matte when you lift the parchment and peek at the surface of the shell. (If the edges brown too quickly, cover the shell with foil.) It doesn't need to color at this point; we are just trying to give the shell a head start in baking before we fill it. When the pie shell is done blind baking, remove it from the oven and let cool on a wire rack, leaving the weights and parchment in place. Leave the oven set at 350°F [175°C].

6. Meanwhile, scrape the pumpkin purée into a medium saucepan. Cook over medium-low heat, stirring occasionally with a wooden spoon, for 30 to 35 minutes, or until the pumpkin reduces into a somewhat-thick paste and darkens in color. Remove from the heat and whisk in the ginger, cinnamon, nutmeg, cloves, and salt. Whisk in the cream, vanilla, and maple syrup until well combined. Whisk in the eggs thoroughly, one by one.

7. Remove the parchment paper and pie weights from the baked shell and pour the pumpkin custard into the shell. Bake for 45 to 55 minutes, or until the custard is just set. The edges of the custard will puff up a little and the center should still have a little wiggle in it. Remove the pie from the oven and let cool on a wire rack for at least 1 hour. Serve at room temperature or chilled, topped with the whipped cream. The pie can be stored, wrapped in plastic wrap, in the refrigerator for up to 3 days.

APPLE-WALNUT-MAPLE CAKE

- 50 g/½ cup walnuts, chopped
- 280 g/2 cups all-purpose flour
- 1 tsp baking powder
- ½ tsp baking soda
- ½ tsp kosher salt
- ½ tsp ground cinnamon
- 3 large eggs, at room temperature
- 160 g/½ cup grade B maple syrup
- 225 g/1 cup unsalted butter, melted and cooled
- 1 Tbsp vanilla extract
- 120 g/½ cup whole milk, at room temperature
- 3 medium Empire, McIntosh, Golden Delicious, Gala, or other sweet baking apples, peeled, cored, and cut into ⅛-in [3-mm] slices

I originally came up with this recipe when testing recipes for a no-sugar baking article for O, the Oprah Magazine. I took some popular recipes from my first and second cookbooks and experimented with substituting various sweeteners for white sugar. This was by far my favorite makeover. In the original recipe for O Magazine, because I was simply tasked with no white sugar, not less sugar in general, the recipe I came up with uses 400 g/1¼ cups of maple syrup. I've learned since that we really don't need as much sweetener as we think we do. So I decreased it by fourths until I got to 160 g/½ cup. You could even go as low as 80 g/¼ cup for more of a breakfast bread than a cake—if you do, increase the milk to 180 g/¾ cup.

1. Place a rack in the center of the oven and preheat to 350°F [175°C]. Butter and flour a 9-in [23-cm] round cake pan or spray with nonstick cooking spray.

2. Put the walnuts on a baking sheet and toast for 8 to 10 minutes, or until lightly toasted. Set aside to cool.

3. In a medium bowl, stir together the flour, baking powder, baking soda, salt, and cinnamon. In a small bowl, whisk together the eggs, maple syrup, butter, vanilla, and milk until thoroughly mixed together. With a rubber spatula, stir the apples and walnuts into the wet ingredients until evenly distributed. Pour the wet ingredients into the dry and fold carefully with a rubber spatula until the wet and dry ingredients are thoroughly incorporated. Be sure there are no flour pockets and also be sure not to over-mix.

4. Pour the batter into the prepared pan. Bake for 50 to 60 minutes, or until the cake is golden brown and springs back when you press it in the center. Remove from the oven and let cool in the pan on a wire rack. Slice and serve. The cake can be stored in an airtight container at room temperature for up to 2 days. Or store in the freezer, tightly wrapped in plastic wrap, for up to 2 weeks; thaw overnight at room temperature before serving.

MAKES

ONE
9-IN [23-CM] CAKE

CHAPTER FIVE

FRUIT IS SWEET

Sometimes when I bite into a juicy, crisp apple, I'm so struck by how perfectly sweet and balanced it is that I wonder why I ever eat anything else. I grew up eating fruit almost exclusively for both snacking and dessert; to this day the inordinate amount of fruit I eat daily should make me the poster child for the USDA food pyramid. Fruit contains fructose to make it sweet. As with any food, you should consume fructose in moderation. But when you're using fruits as your sweetener, you can know that you are adding flavor and sweetness naturally to make these desserts delicious and memorable.

WALNUT CRUST

- 100 g/1 cup walnuts, finely chopped
- 140 g/1 cup all-purpose flour
- ¼ tsp kosher salt
- 2 tsp ground cinnamon
- 85 g/6 Tbsp unsalted butter, melted and cooled
- 120 g/½ cup whole milk
- 1 Tbsp vanilla extract

PUMPKIN CHEESECAKE FILLING

- One 335-g/12-oz can frozen apple juice concentrate, thawed
- 240 g/1 cup pitted and finely chopped Medjool dates
- ½ tsp baking soda
- 340 g/12 oz cream cheese, at room temperature
- 120 g/½ cup heavy cream
- 420 g/15 oz pumpkin purée
- 3 large eggs
- 2 Tbsp vanilla extract
- 1 tsp ground cinnamon
- 1 tsp ground ginger
- ¼ tsp freshly grated nutmeg
- ⅛ tsp ground cloves
- ½ tsp kosher salt

PUMPKIN-WALNUT CHEESECAKE BARS

It's a shame that we typically eat pumpkin pie only once a year at Thanksgiving. I always take one bite and think: I want to eat this all the time! For a flash, you see them in bakeries and grocery stores and then WHOOF! they're gone. Here's a way to enjoy all of the warm, spicy flavors of a terrific pumpkin pie in cheesecake form. A simple walnut crust is topped with creamy, gently spiced pumpkin cheesecake filling and baked until just set.

1. Place a rack in the center of the oven and preheat to 350°F [175°C]. Butter the bottom of a 9-by-13-in [23-by-33-cm] baking pan, or butter and line the bottom with parchment paper.

2. To make the crust: Put the walnuts on a baking sheet and toast for 8 to 10 minutes, or until lightly toasted. Set aside to cool.

3. In a medium bowl, use a wooden spoon to stir together the walnuts, flour, salt, and cinnamon. Drizzle the butter over the flour mixture and stir to mix in. In a small bowl, combine the milk and vanilla and add to the flour mixture; stir until the dough comes together. It will be very soft. Press the dough evenly on the bottom of the prepared pan and bake for 15 to 18 minutes, or until it is no longer wet looking and starts to turn pale golden brown. Remove from the oven and let cool completely on a wire rack.

MAKES

16

BARS

4. Meanwhile, make the filling: In a medium saucepan, bring the apple juice concentrate to a boil over high heat and then decrease the heat to medium-low and simmer until the juice reduces to ¾ cup [180 ml], 20 to 30 minutes. It will thicken up, become syrupy, and boil a little slower as it reduces. Watch out that it does not over-boil or burn; you may need to decrease the heat as it thickens. To check to see if it is reduced enough, every now and then pour the juice into a measuring cup to measure it; if it is not yet ¾ cup [180 ml], pour it back into the saucepan to continue to simmer and reduce until it measures out to ¾ cup [180 ml]. Remove from the heat and set aside.

5. While the juice is reducing, put the dates and baking soda in a small bowl and add enough hot water to cover the dates. Stir to dissolve the baking soda; it will soften the skins of the dates, allowing them to blend more easily into the filling. Let the dates soak for 10 to 15 minutes. Drain the dates and, using a spoon, mash them until they are smooth and soft. Mix the mashed dates into the reduced juice and refrigerate until cold to the touch.

6. With a food processor, blend the cream cheese, reduced apple juice and dates, and cream for 2 to 3 minutes, or until the dates mix into the cream cheese. Add the pumpkin, eggs, vanilla, cinnamon, ginger, nutmeg, cloves, and salt and process for 2 to 3 minutes, or until well blended, stopping occasionally to scrape the sides with a rubber spatula. Pour the pumpkin mixture on top of the baked crust.

7. Bake for 40 to 50 minutes, or until the top of the filling is set and doesn't jiggle when you wiggle the pan. Remove from the oven and let cool to room temperature on a wire rack. Refrigerate for at least 3 hours to chill. Cut into 16 bars and serve. Bars can be stored in an airtight container in the refrigerator for up to 5 days.

- 100 g/1 cup pecans, chopped
- 160 g/⅔ cup pitted and finely chopped Medjool dates
- ¼ tsp baking soda
- 225 g/1 cup cold unsalted butter, cut into ½-in [1-cm] pieces
- 1 Tbsp vanilla extract
- 1 egg yolk
- ½ tsp kosher salt
- 210 g/1½ cups all-purpose flour
- 30 g/¼ cup cornstarch

PECAN-DATE SHORTBREAD COOKIES

These tender, melt-in-your-mouth, just-barely sweet shortbread cookies will have you stocking your pantry with dates so you can make these over and over again. Dates offer a rich, caramelized sweetness to pastries in much the same way brown sugar does. Soak them in a little baking soda before you mash them into a sweet paste—the baking soda breaks down the sometimes leathery skin and renders it soft enough to dissolve into the cookie dough.

1. Place a rack in the center of the oven and preheat to 350°F [175°C].

2. Put the pecans on a baking sheet and toast for 8 to 10 minutes, until lightly toasted. Set aside to cool.

3. Put the dates and baking soda in a small bowl and add enough hot water to cover the dates. Stir to dissolve the baking soda; it will soften the skins of the dates. Let the dates soak for 10 to 15 minutes. Drain the dates and, using a spoon, mash them until they are smooth and soft.

4. Using a stand mixer fitted with the paddle attachment (or with an electric hand mixer or by hand with a wooden spoon), beat the butter and dates on medium speed for about 5 minutes, or until light and fluffy. Beat in the vanilla, egg yolk, and salt until thoroughly combined. Scrape the bowl down with a rubber spatula to make sure all of the yolk is mixed in with the butter-date mixture.

5. In a medium bowl, stir together the flour, cornstarch, and pecans. In three or four increments, blend the flour mixture into the butter-date mixture on low speed. Mix until the flour is totally blended in and the dough is homogenous. Make sure to scrape the bowl down again with a rubber spatula during mixing to ensure that all the flour is thoroughly incorporated.

Continued

MAKES

12

COOKIES

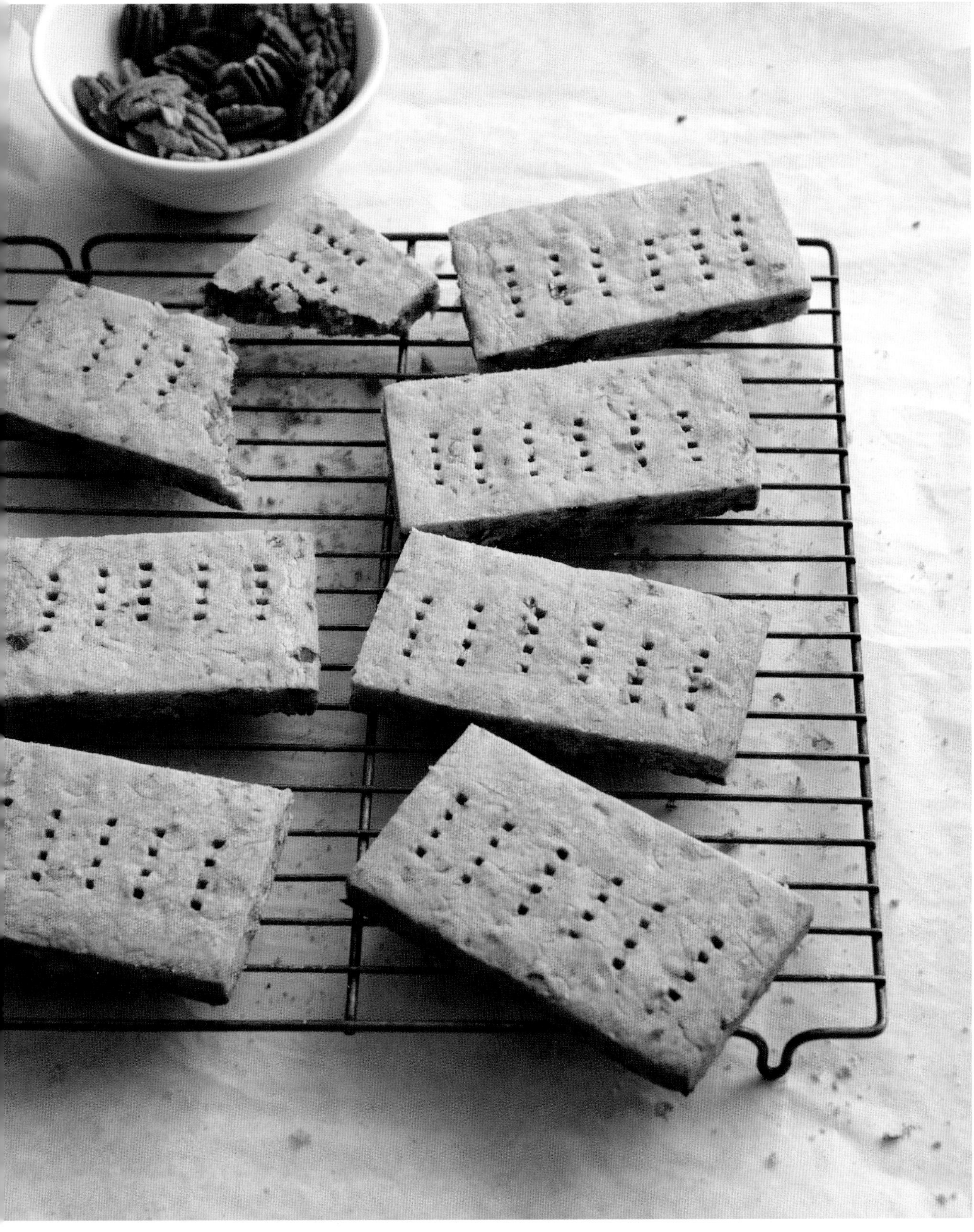

6. Scrape the dough onto a piece of parchment paper. Press the dough together and, using your hands, form it into a rough rectangle. Switch to a rolling pin, sprinkle the pin and the dough with flour to keep it from sticking, and roll the dough into a rectangle about 8 by 12 in [20 by 30 cm] and ¼ in [6 mm] thick. Transfer the dough and parchment paper to a baking sheet. Using a sharp knife, cut the dough in half lengthwise, and then cut each half into six pieces, so you end up with twelve rectangular cookies. With a fork, poke a few decorative holes in a line down the middle of each cookie.

7. Bake for 30 to 35 minutes, or until the shortbread is pale golden brown and baked through. Remove from the oven and let cool completely on the baking sheet on a wire rack. Cut along the knife marks to separate the cookies and serve. Shortbread can be stored in an airtight container for up to 5 days.

SPICED PEAR TURNOVERS

- 1 recipe Quick Puff Pastry (page 164)
- 1 recipe Spiced Pear Compote (page 165)
- 1 large egg
- 2 Tbsp heavy cream

If you are nervous about making puff pastry, don't be. These turnovers use an easy and straightforward variation of traditional puff pastry called quick puff. The pear compote is gently sweetened with dates and spices, and they infuse the turnovers with their heady scent; the puff bakes flaky and buttery, and you'll not only impress your family and friends but also yourself at how divine these pastries are.

1. Place a rack in the center of the oven and preheat to 350°F [175°C]. Line a baking sheet with parchment paper.

2. On a well-floured work surface, roll the puff pastry into a rectangle about 31 by 13 in [79 by 33 cm]. The dough may seem pretty tough and difficult to roll out at first. Don't be afraid to be firm with the dough: flip it upside down, turn it side to side, and pound it with the rolling pin to flatten it as you roll it into a long rectangle. Using a sharp knife, trim the edges of the rectangle to get rid of any rough edges so your final rectangle is 30 by 12 in [76 by 30 cm]. Now, cut the dough into 10 equal squares: First, halve the dough lengthwise into two strips, each 6 by 30 in [15 by 76 cm], and then cut each strip into five 6-in [15-cm] squares. Use a ruler or a straight edge to measure the squares exactly so that the turnovers are easier to fill and the final pastry is uniform in size and appearance.

Continued

MAKES

10

TURNOVERS

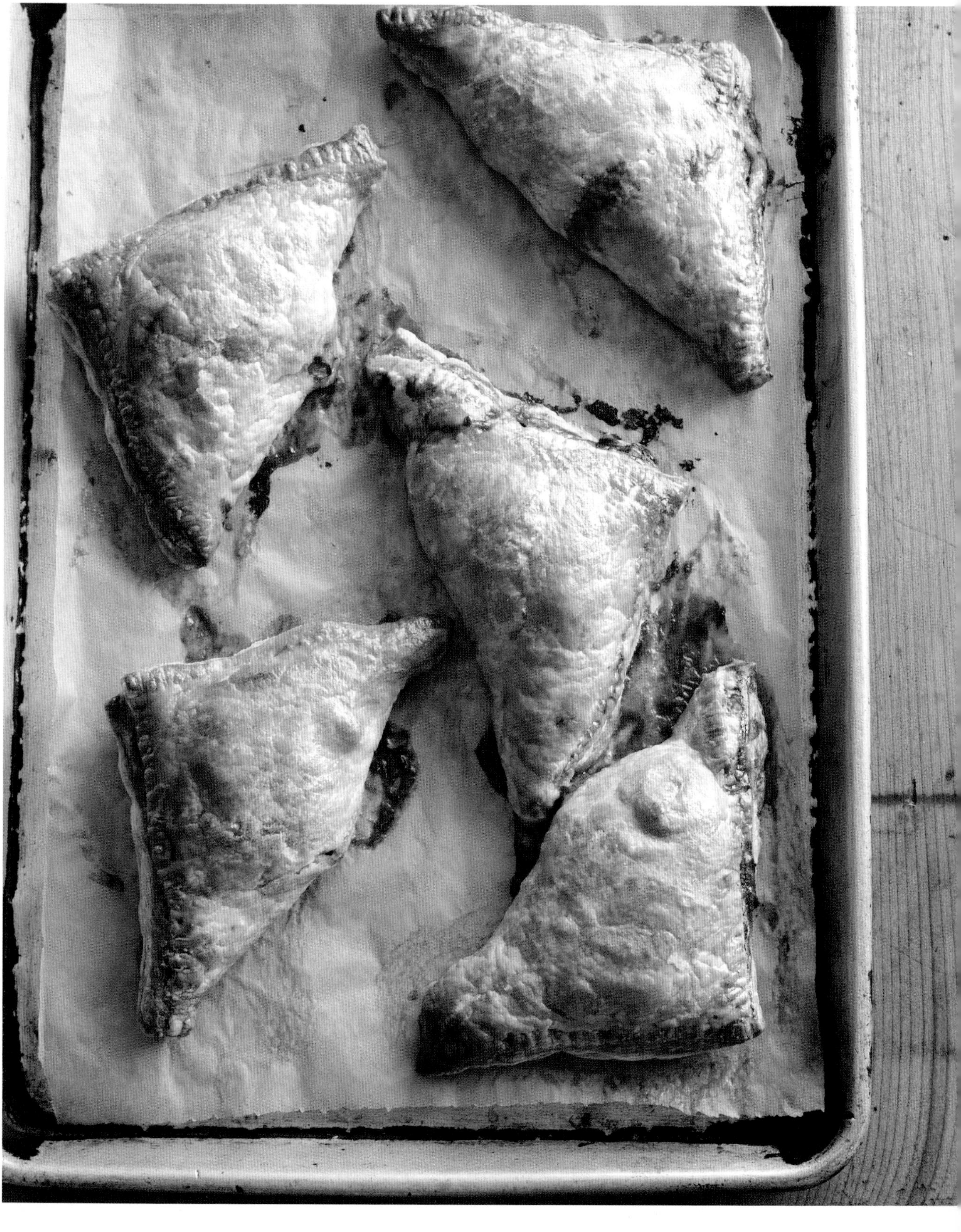

3. Place about ⅓ cup [80 g] of the pear compote on one side of each square and spread the compote a little so it fills half of the square diagonally. Use the back of a spoon to spread it evenly and leave a little bit of a lip around the filling to allow for the sealing of the dough triangle. Break the egg into a small bowl and whisk it with a fork; using a pastry brush, brush the exposed pastry dough with the egg wash. Carefully fold the egg-washed dough over the compote, and use your fingers to pinch the turnover triangle together. Use the tines of the fork to firmly press the edges of the turnover together and make sure the turnover is well sealed. Continue with all of the dough squares and compote.

4. At this point the unbaked turnovers can be stored in the freezer, individually wrapped in plastic wrap, for up to 2 weeks. You can bake them directly from the freezer; add 5 to 8 minutes to the baking time and proceed as directed.

5. Transfer the turnovers to the prepared baking sheet. Add the cream to the remaining egg wash and whisk with a fork. Using a pastry brush, brush the tops of the turnovers with the egg-cream mixture. Bake for about 1 hour, or until the dough is entirely browned and baked through. Look at the sides of the turnovers where the puff pastry has poofed up to make sure this part of the turnover is golden brown as well. Remove from the oven and let cool on the baking sheet on a wire rack for at least 1 hour before serving to allow the filling to cool. The turnovers are best enjoyed the same day you bake them, but they can be stored in an airtight container at room temperature for up to 2 days; refresh them in a 300°F [150°C] oven for 6 to 8 minutes.

QUICK PUFF PASTRY

MAKES ABOUT 1½ LB [680 G] DOUGH

- 280 g/2 cups all-purpose flour
- 1 tsp kosher salt
- 340 g/1½ cups cold unsalted butter, cut into ½-in [1-cm] cubes
- 80 g/⅓ cup ice water

1. Using a stand mixer fitted with the paddle attachment (or with an electric hand mixer), combine the flour and salt. Toss in the cubes of butter and pulse the mixer on and off on the lowest speed for 45 seconds to 1 minute, or until the butter is broken down into pieces the size of small marbles. Pour in the ice water and mix for 10 to 15 seconds, or just until everything comes together in a shaggy and rough-looking dough. It will start out looking like crumbs and floury butter, and then turn into more of a rough and shaggy dough as you beat it.

2. Dump out the dough onto a generously floured work surface and pat it into a rough 8-in [20-cm] square. Using a rolling pin, roll the dough from left to right as well as you can into a rectangle about 18 by 8 in [46 by 20 cm] and ½ in [1 cm] thick. Flour the dough as needed to prevent the rolling pin from sticking. Don't worry if it seems really messy and not at all smooth. Just do your best to roll the square shape into a rectangle.

3. Lightly score the rectangle into thirds with a bench scraper or knife. Each third should be roughly 6 in [13 cm] wide and still 8 in [20 cm] from top to bottom. Brush off any loose flour from the dough. Take the right third of the dough and, as best you can, flip it over onto the middle third. Then take the left third of the dough and, again as best you can, flip that third on top of the middle

and right third. You should now have a messy pile of dough about 6 by 8 in [13 by 20 cm] and about 2 in [5 cm] thick. Turn the entire dough pile as best as you can 90 degrees clockwise so that now it is 8 in [20 cm] side to side and 6 in [13 cm] up and down. (This process—folding the dough in thirds and then rotating it 90 degrees—is called turning the dough.) The dough should still be rough looking and you'll see bits of butter throughout.

4. Once again, roll this out into a rectangle about 18 by 8 in [46 by 20 cm]. This time the dough should be a little more cohesive, and you should find it a little easier to roll it out. Make sure your work surface and dough are well floured. Do your best to roll the dough into as even a rectangle as you can with sharp corners.

5. When rolling out laminated dough like puff pastry, your goal is to keep the layers directly on top of one another and even, to preserve the layering. In between turns you have three layers of dough, one on top of another. Rather than immediately rolling these out with a back-and-forth motion, first flatten the dough with your rolling pin by firmly pressing down on the dough and then moving your rolling pin up and down and pounding along the length of the dough—use your rolling pin to create ridges as it compacts the dough. Once the dough is pressed down all over, then use the pin to roll back and forth, smoothing out the ridges while flattening and rolling the dough into the shape you want. By pressing down first before rolling, you preserve the layers. If you were to start rolling immediately after folding the dough, the very top layer would take all the pressure from the rolling pin and stretch out way over the very bottom layer. Using this technique to compress the dough first helps to keep the layers even, making for a flakier end product.

6. Again, give the dough a turn by dividing it into thirds, flipping the right third into the middle, and then the left third on top of that (it's like folding a business letter), and then turning the entire piece of dough 90 degrees. Dust off any loose flour in between folds.

7. Repeat this process twice more, for a total of four turns. By the time you get to the fourth turn, the dough should be completely cohesive and almost smooth. There may be small chunks of butter in it, but it should no longer be shaggy and difficult to work with.

8. Place the dough on a baking sheet and cover it completely with plastic wrap, tucking the plastic under the dough as if you're tucking it into bed. Refrigerate for 1 to 2 hours.

9. Remove the dough from the refrigerator and place it on a work surface with the long side of the rectangle close to you. Turn the dough as described (roll it out into a long rectangle, fold it in thirds, then rotate it 90 degrees) twice more. Flip the dough over occasionally during the rolling process to make sure the top and bottom layers are getting equal attention from the rolling pin. When you are finished, the dough will have gone through six turns total—four initially and then two more after resting in the refrigerator.

10. The puff pastry dough is now finished but needs to rest before you can use it. Wrap the dough in plastic wrap and refrigerate for at least 1 hour or up to 2 days. Or store in the freezer, well wrapped in plastic wrap, for up to 1 month. Pull the dough out the night before you plan to use it and thaw in the refrigerator.

SPICED PEAR COMPOTE

MAKES ABOUT 3½ CUPS [840 G], ENOUGH FOR ABOUT 10 TURNOVERS

- 120 g/½ cup pitted and finely chopped Medjool dates
- ¼ tsp baking soda
- 3 Tbsp unsalted butter
- 5 or 6 ripe medium Bosc pears, peeled, cored, and chopped into small dice
- 2 tsp vanilla extract
- 1 tsp ground cinnamon
- 1 tsp ground ginger
- ¼ tsp ground allspice
- Pinch of ground cloves
- ¼ tsp kosher salt

Put the dates and baking soda in a small bowl and add enough hot water to cover the dates. Stir to dissolve the baking soda; it will soften the skins of the dates allowing them to blend more easily into the pears. Let the dates soak for 10 to 15 minutes. Drain the dates and, using a spoon, mash them until they are smooth and soft. In a large skillet, melt the butter over medium heat and add the dates, pears, vanilla, cinnamon, ginger, allspice, cloves, and salt. Cook for 5 to 6 minutes, or until the dates and pears are starting to soften and the spices are well distributed. Add up to ¼ cup [60 ml] water if the pears seem dry and cook for 5 to 6 minutes more. You want the dates to dissolve into the pears and the pears to soften somewhat, so keep cooking for another few minutes, adding a bit more water if needed, until you have a soft pear compote. Remove from the heat and let cool. The compote can be stored in an airtight container in the refrigerator for up to 1 week.

- One 335-g/12-oz can frozen apple juice concentrate, thawed
- 225 g/8 oz cream cheese, at room temperature
- 120 g/½ cup crème fraîche (see page 24)
- 480 g/2 cups heavy cream
- 2 tsp vanilla extract
- ⅛ tsp kosher salt
- 520 g/4 cups strawberries, hulled and quartered (halved if the berries are small)

STRAWBERRY CREAM CHEESE FOOL

Christopher never met a dessert that he didn't like. Neither have I, for that matter. But I knew he must have tried something really special when he came home one night and raved about a blueberry fool that he had at our friend Esti's restaurant, Sam's. Rich, creamy cream cheese, jammy sweet blueberries, wedges of shortbread. It was like the best blueberry pie you'd ever eaten, deconstructed. I finally made my way over to Sam's to taste it and agreed with him that it was divine. I knew I'd love it more if I could create a less-sweet version. This fool uses reduced apple juice to sweeten the fluffy cream cheese, and fresh strawberries are folded in at the last minute to make a delightful creamy, easy dessert.

1. In a small saucepan, bring the apple juice concentrate to a boil over medium-high heat. Decrease the heat to medium-low and simmer for 15 to 20 minutes, or until the juice reduces to ¾ cup [180 ml]. It will thicken up, become syrupy, and boil a little slower as it reduces. Watch out that it does not over-boil or burn; you may need to decrease the heat as it thickens. To check to see if it is reduced enough, every now and then pour the juice into a measuring cup to measure it; if it is not ¾ cup [180 ml] pour it back into the saucepan to continue to simmer and reduce until it measures out to ¾ cup [180 ml]. Remove from the heat and cool in the refrigerator until cold to the touch.

Continued

SERVES

8 TO 10

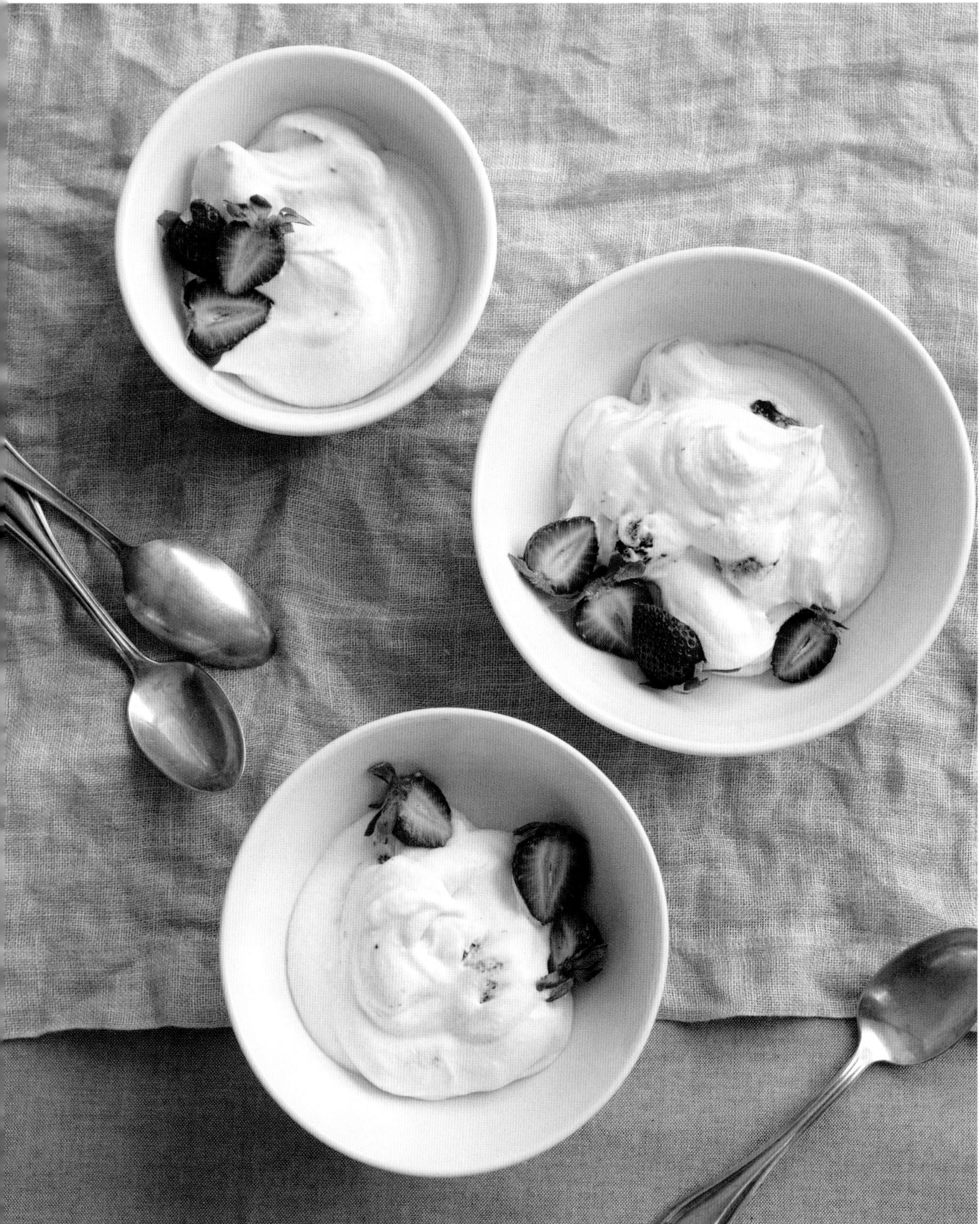

2. Using a stand mixer fitted with the whisk attachment (or with an electric hand mixer), whip together the cream cheese and 1/2 cup [120 ml] of the reduced apple juice concentrate (reserve the rest of the apple juice for another use or discard) on medium speed for 2 to 3 minutes, or until the mixture is light and fluffy, scraping the bowl occasionally with a rubber spatula to get all of the cream cheese whipped up. Add the crème fraîche and whip together to combine. Slowly drizzle in the cream and beat, still on medium speed, for 1 to 2 minutes more, or until the cream thickens and combines with the cream cheese mixture. Whisk in the vanilla and salt.

3. Fold the strawberries into the cream cheese mixture, saving a few spoonfuls of berries to garnish the top of the fools. Portion the fools into bowls or glasses and top each with a generous spoonful of strawberries. Serve immediately or cover with plastic wrap and refrigerate for up to 2 hours.

COCONUT TAPIOCA
WITH PINEAPPLE, MANGO, AND LIME

- 480 g/2 cups whole milk
- One 380-g/13.5-oz can unsweetened coconut milk
- 2 tsp vanilla extract
- 80 g/½ cup small pearl tapioca
- ¼ pineapple, peeled, cored, and cut into small dice, or one 225-g/8-oz can pineapple chunks, in their own juices, chopped into smaller pieces
- One 335-g/12-oz can frozen apple juice concentrate, thawed
- 1 vanilla bean
- ¼ tsp kosher salt
- 1 large or 2 small mangoes, peeled, pitted, and diced
- Finely grated zest and juice of 1 lime

Creamy coconut tapioca pudding with glazed pineapple is one of the desserts I obsessed over when I lived in New York City and worked for François Payard. All of the cooks at Payard Patisserie spent our free time talking about the places we dreamed of going and the dishes we couldn't wait to try. One of the cooks told me about how Claudia Fleming, at the time the pastry chef at Gramercy Tavern, had created a dreamy tapioca that could not be missed. He was right—on one of my last nights in NYC, I was finally able to try it, and thereafter every time I went to visit NYC, I made a point of going back to order it again. Sadly, it's no longer on the menu, but I've channeled it here in this version. It's light and refreshing and uses the natural sugars of mango, pineapple, and apple juice to complement the richness of the coconut milk.

1. In a small saucepan, combine the milk, coconut milk, and vanilla and bring to a gentle simmer over medium-low heat. Stir in the tapioca, decrease the heat to low, and cook, stirring occasionally, for about 30 minutes, or until the tapioca is softened. The tapioca will become translucent and will no longer have a white center when it is fully cooked.

2. Meanwhile, put the pineapple (either fresh or canned with juice) and the apple juice concentrate in a medium saucepan and bring to a boil over medium-high heat. Using a small paring knife, split the vanilla bean in half lengthwise, and scrape the seeds into the juice.

Continued

SERVES

4 OR 5

3. Decrease the heat to medium-low and simmer the juice and fruit for 20 to 25 minutes, or until the juice becomes thick and syrupy. It will thicken up and boil a little slower as it reduces. Watch out that it does not over-boil or burn; you may need to decrease the heat as it thickens. Remove from the heat and strain the pineapple from the juice. Put the pineapple in a bowl and refrigerate until chilled.

4. Remove the tapioca from the heat and stir in the reduced juice and the salt. Transfer the tapioca mixture to a bowl, cover lightly with plastic wrap, and refrigerate until it cools completely, at least 3 hours or up to overnight.

5. Right before serving, fold about half of the diced mango and the lime juice into the tapioca. Divide the pudding evenly into clear glasses. Fold the remaining mango into the reserved chopped pineapple. Spoon the fruit on top of the pudding to cover in an even layer. Garnish with a little grated lime zest. Serve immediately.

- 240 g/1½ cups whole natural (unblanched) almonds
- 180 g/¾ cup pitted and chopped Medjool dates
- ½ tsp baking soda
- ½ tsp vanilla extract
- ¼ tsp almond extract
- ½ tsp kosher salt
- 2½ tsp granulated unflavored gelatin

PLUM-GRAPE COMPOTE

- 3 medium black or red plums, halved, pitted, and thinly sliced
- 60 g/¼ cup frozen grape juice concentrate (defrost to measure)
- 80 g/½ cup seedless red or green grapes, halved
- ¼ tsp almond extract

ALMOND MILK PANNA COTTA
WITH PLUM-GRAPE COMPOTE

Growing up, we so rarely had dessert (unless you count a plate of oranges . . . whoo-weee, what a TREAT!) that on the very few occasions when my mom actually made something sweet, it was cause for amazement and wonder in my brother and me. Known as "almond jelly" or "almond tofu," this popular Taiwanese treat is a Jell-O–like custard usually seen in rolling carts at dim sum restaurants. Sometimes it's made with agar-agar and sometimes with soy milk. My mom made hers old-school style, with gelatin, milk, sugar, and almond extract and topped it with Del Monte fruit cocktail; we called it white Jell-O. Both the making of it with Mom and eating it with my brother are among my favorite childhood food memories. I wanted to re-create a no-sugar version that also was dairy-free by making my own almond milk. The dates sweeten the homemade almond milk just enough, and you use just a smidge of almond extract to accentuate the almond flavor. Instead of canned fruits in heavy syrup, these light, refreshing custards are topped with a simple plum and grape compote mixed with a little grape juice.

SERVES

4

1. Soak the almonds in 3 cups [720 ml] cold water overnight at room temperature in a covered container. Drain the almonds the next day and place in a blender with 3 cups [720 ml] fresh cold water. Put the dates and baking soda in a small bowl and add enough hot water to cover the dates. Stir to dissolve the baking soda; it will soften the skins of the dates, allowing them to blend more easily into the almonds. Let the dates soak for 10 to 15 minutes. Drain the dates and add to the blender. Whir in the blender for 3 full minutes on high speed. Line a fine-mesh strainer with cheese-cloth and set it over a 4-cup [960-ml] measuring cup. Strain through the lined strainer into the measuring cup. Squeeze the almond meal to get all of the milk out of the almonds—you should get 2½ to 3 cups [600 to 720 ml] almond milk. Add the vanilla, almond extract, and salt and stir well.

2. Remove about ½ cup [120 ml] of the almond milk, place in a medium bowl, and evenly sprinkle with the gelatin to soften it. (This is called blooming the gelatin and will allow it to properly dissolve in the rest of the liquid.) Warm the remaining almond milk in a small saucepan over medium heat until it is hot to the touch and stir it into the softened gelatin until the gelatin completely dissolves. Divide into 4 serving bowls or cups. Refrigerate, covered with plastic wrap, for at least 3 hours, or up to 4 days.

3. Meanwhile, make the compote: In a small saucepan over medium heat, simmer the plums with the grape juice concentrate for 15 to 20 minutes, or until the plums are softened and the juice thickens a bit. Remove from the heat and stir in the grapes. Add the almond extract and let cool. The compote can be stored in an airtight container in the refrigerator for up to 1 week.

4. Spoon the compote over the chilled panna cottas and serve.

- 1.4 kg/6 cups orange juice (preferably freshly squeezed)
- 420 g/1¾ cups apple juice
- ½ vanilla bean or 2 tsp vanilla extract
- 120 g/½ cup water
- 2 ripe medium Anjou, Bartlett, or other soft, sweet pears, peeled, cored, and cut into eighths
- 160 g/1 cup dried cranberries
- 1 ruby red grapefruit
- 2 seedless oranges
- 6 to 8 fresh mint leaves, thinly sliced (optional)

ORANGE GRANITA
WITH PEARS, CRANBERRIES, AND CITRUS

Light and refreshing, this pretty, elegant dessert is a cinch to put together. Because both the granita and the pears are made in advance, it is also easy to prepare ahead of time. The granita is stored in the freezer and the poached pears in the refrigerator, allowing you to pull all together as a last-minute dessert for friends and family. I've suggested my favorite fall fruits to go with the orange granita, but feel free to substitute other fruits as you wish. I've made this with apples, apricots, and grapes as well as with quince, figs, and raspberries.

1. In a medium saucepan, bring the orange juice to a boil over medium-high heat. Decrease the heat to medium and boil gently, stirring occasionally, for 45 minutes, or until reduced by half. Stir in 180 g/¾ cup of the apple juice and let cool to room temperature. Transfer to a freezer-proof, airtight container and freeze for at least 8 hours or up to overnight. (The granita can be made up to 2 weeks in advance and stored in the freezer.)

2. With a paring knife, split the vanilla bean lengthwise down the middle and scrape out the seeds into a small saucepan. (If using vanilla extract, add it later, along with the fruit.) Whisk in the remaining 240 g/ 1 cup apple juice and the water and bring just to a boil over medium-high heat. Remove from the heat and add the pears and cranberries (and vanilla extract, if using), submerging them in the poaching liquid. Cover and set aside for 1 hour, then transfer to an airtight container and refrigerate until cold, at least 4 hours. (The fruit may be made up to a week in advance and stored in the refrigerator.)

Continued

SERVES

6 TO 8

3. Remove the granita from the freezer and set aside at room temperature for 15 minutes, or until scraping a spoon across the surface produces crystalline ice shavings. Meanwhile, cut off the skin and pith of the grapefruit and oranges. Using a sharp knife, cut between the pith and remove the citrus segments. Mix into the chilled poached fruits. Transfer the ice shavings to bowls and, using a slotted spoon, arrange some fruit on top of each serving. (Save the poaching liquid for another use such as mixing with seltzer water and ice for a refreshing light drink, if you'd like.) Garnish with the mint (if using) and serve immediately.

PINEAPPLE-COCONUT-BANANA SORBET

- One 335-g/12-oz can frozen pineapple juice concentrate, thawed
- One 380-g/13.5-oz can unsweetened coconut milk
- 2 ripe bananas
- 120 g/½ cup water
- ½ tsp vanilla extract
- ½ tsp kosher salt

This tropical sorbet is about as easy and delicious a recipe as can be. All you need is an ice cream maker and you're moments away from diving into a naturally sweet and lusciously creamy dessert. For a grown-up variation, add 3 to 4 Tbsp dark rum and pretend you are soaking up rays on a sunny beach in the Caribbean. I've made this without the bananas as well when they haven't been ripe enough, and my husband, Christopher, actually prefers the banana-free version. Try both yourself and see which you like best.

1. In a blender or a food processor, combine the pineapple concentrate, coconut milk, bananas, water, vanilla, and salt and blend until the bananas are totally mixed in. (Alternatively, mash up the bananas by hand and mix them into the remaining ingredients, whisking well to thoroughly combine.)

2. Churn in an ice cream maker according to the manufacturer's directions. When the sorbet has finished churning, either enjoy right away or transfer to an airtight container and freeze for up to 1 week. Remove from the freezer for 10 to 15 minutes before serving to soften it up for scooping.

MAKES ABOUT

1½

QUARTS [1.4L]

- 6 ripe bananas, peeled and frozen
- 120 g/½ cup heavy cream
- 2 tsp vanilla extract
- ¼ tsp kosher salt
- Pinch of ground cinnamon

UNBELIEVABLE BANANA ICE CREAM

I've always loved a frozen ripe banana as a quick and healthy pick-me-up for its natural sweetness and creaminess. Peel a ripe banana, put it in a resealable plastic bag, freeze until hard, and enjoy your sweet fruit Popsicle. It just takes a few extra steps to turn this simple treat into a more decadent creamy ice cream that rivals the finest premium stuff. As a bonus, you'll know that you're eating something that is good for you to boot. This ice cream is best served within a few hours of blending, at which point it has a lovely soft-serve consistency, but you can definitely make it in advance and store it in the freezer like regular ice cream as well.

Cut the bananas into ½-in [1-cm] slices and place in a blender. Pour in the cream and vanilla and blend on high speed until smooth. Add the salt and cinnamon and blend again. The ice cream may be enjoyed immediately or stored in an airtight container in the freezer for up to 2 weeks. Remove from the freezer and let soften for 10 to 15 minutes at room temperature before serving.

MAKES ABOUT

1

QUART [960 ML]

SUMMER PEACH DUMPLINGS
WITH ALMONDS AND WHIPPED CREAM

- One 335-g/12-oz can frozen apple juice concentrate, thawed
- 3 Tbsp softened unsalted butter, plus 55 g/4 Tbsp cold unsalted butter, cut into small pieces
- 1/8 tsp kosher salt, plus 1/4 tsp
- 175 g/1 1/4 cups all-purpose flour
- 50 g/1/2 cup almond flour
- 1 tsp baking powder
- 1/4 tsp baking soda
- 120 g/1/2 cup cold buttermilk
- 1/4 tsp almond extract
- 3 ripe medium peaches, peeled
- 2 Tbsp heavy cream plus 1/2 cup (120 ml) whipped to soft peaks, for garnish
- 25 g/1/4 cup sliced almonds

I'm so enamored with the flaky pie dough that we use for everything at Flour that I sometimes forget about all of the other amazing pastry doughs out there, like this biscuit dough. Who doesn't love biting into a warm, fluffy biscuit slathered with butter and jam? You'll love this even more: Start with ripe fragrant peaches, wrap them in buttery biscuit dough, and bake them with reduced apple juice to help add sweetness and tart flavor. The almonds not only highlight the peachy flavors but also add great crunch to the dumplings.

1. In a small saucepan, bring the apple juice concentrate to a boil over medium-high heat, decrease the heat to medium-low, and simmer the juice for 10 to 12 minutes, or until it reduces to about 1 cup [240 ml]. To check to see if it is reduced enough, every now and then pour the juice into a measuring cup to measure it; if it is not 1 cup [240 ml], pour it back into the saucepan to continue to simmer and reduce until it measures out to 1 cup [240 ml]. Remove from the heat and whisk in 2 Tbsp of the softened butter and the 1/8 tsp salt. Set aside.

2. Using a stand mixer fitted with the paddle attachment (or with an electric hand mixer), briefly mix the all-purpose flour, almond flour, baking powder, baking soda, and the 1/4 tsp salt on low speed until combined. Add the cold butter pieces and beat on low speed for about 1 minute, or until the butter is mixed in and pea-sized and the dough looks like coarse meal. (Alternatively, use a pastry cutter or two knives to cut the butter into the dry ingredients; proceed as directed. Use a wooden spoon to mix the wet ingredients into the dry ingredients.)

Continued

MAKES

6

DUMPLINGS

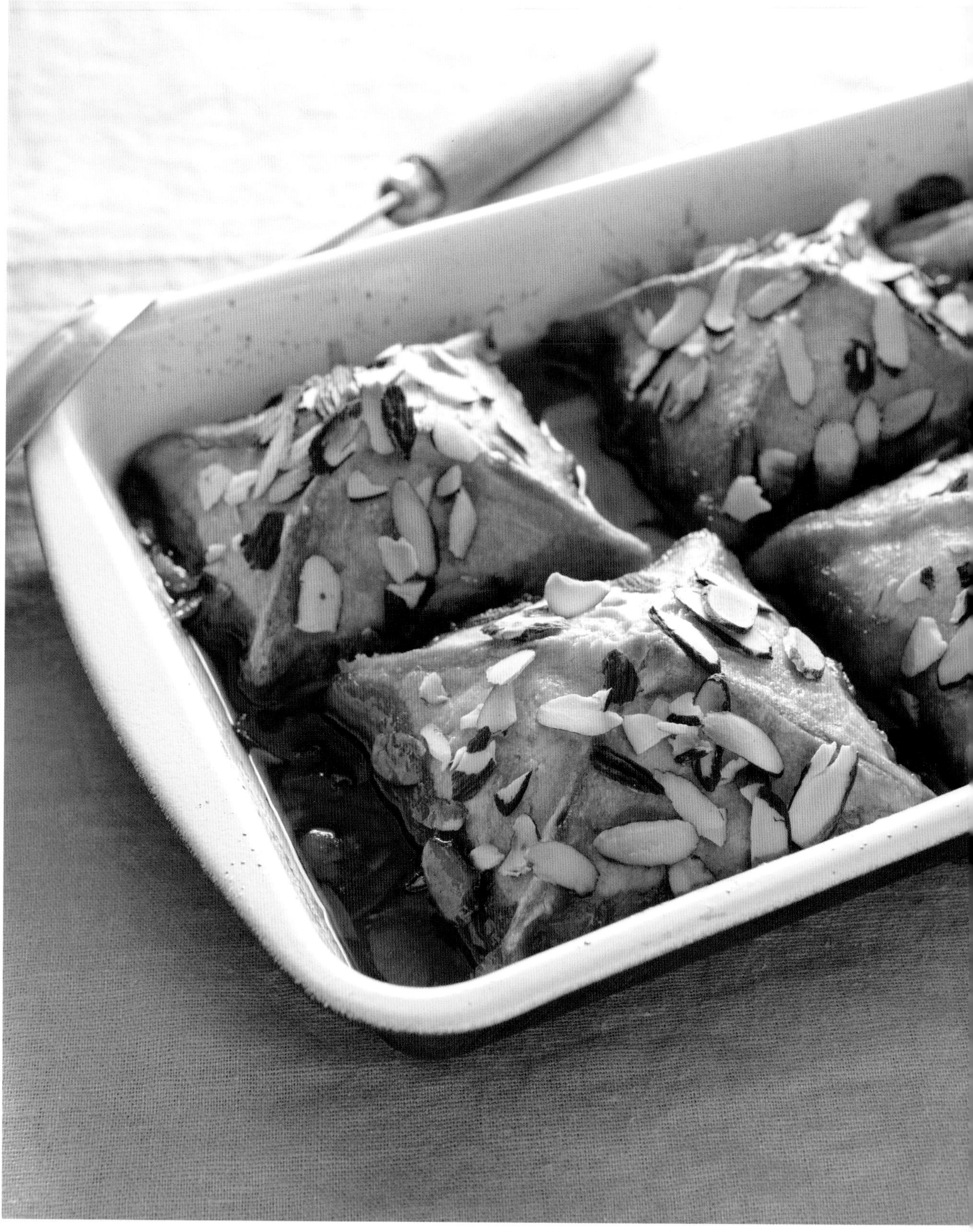

3. In a small bowl, whisk together the buttermilk and almond extract. With the mixer on low speed, pour the buttermilk into the flour-butter mixture and beat for 10 to 20 seconds, or until the dough comes together. It will be very soft. Wrap the dough loosely in plastic wrap and refrigerate for at least 40 minutes or up to 2 days.

4. Place a rack in the center of the oven and pre-heat to 350°F [175°C].

5. Halve and pit the peaches. Remove the chilled dough from the refrigerator. On a well-floured work surface, roll out the dough into a rectangle about 10 in [25 cm] by 15 in [38 cm]. Cut the dough in half lengthwise and then in thirds widthwise, forming six 5-in [13-cm] squares. Place a peach half, cut-side down, in the center of a dough square; pinch off a bit of the remaining 1 Tbsp softened butter and smear it on top of the peach. Gently stretch the four corners of the dough upward and gather them together at the top of the peach, pinching the dough along the seams to seal into a dumpling. Repeat with the rest of the peaches and dough squares. Place the dumplings, seam-side up, in a 9-by-13-in [23-by-33-cm] baking pan and brush them with the 2 Tbsp cream. Sprinkle the dumplings evenly with the almonds.

6. Pour the apple juice–butter mixture into the bottom of the baking pan around the dumplings. Bake the dumplings for 30 to 40 minutes, or until the dumplings are golden brown. Remove from the oven and let cool in the pan on a wire rack for 15 minutes. When the dumplings are cool enough to handle, use a spatula to place them on serving plates with dollops of whipped cream and any extra syrup from the baking pan. The dumplings are best served warm the day you make them.

- 175 g/1¼ cups all-purpose flour, plus 45 g/5 Tbsp
- 1 tsp baking powder
- ¼ tsp baking soda
- Kosher salt
- 2¼ tsp ground cinnamon
- 115 g/½ cup cold unsalted butter, cut into 8 to 10 pieces, plus 2 Tbsp unsalted butter, at room temperature
- 2 egg yolks
- 360 g/1½ cups crème fraîche (see page 24)
- 1 Tbsp vanilla extract
- One 335-g/12-oz can frozen grape juice concentrate, thawed
- 260 g/2 cups fresh blueberries
- 260 g/2 cups fresh raspberries
- 260 g/2 cups fresh blackberries
- 260 g/2 cups fresh strawberries, hulled and quartered
- 1 tsp freshly squeezed lemon juice
- 60 g/¼ cup heavy cream

MIXED BERRY COBBLER
WITH CRÈME FRAÎCHE

One of the goals of this book was to see if, with the right recipes, I could train your palate to enjoy—fully enjoy—desserts made with less to no sugar. I made two versions of this cobbler for some good friends who came over for dinner in the middle of my testing. They had been willing guinea pigs for this book many times over already, offering their honest opinions with each recipe (and sending me back into the kitchen more times than I can count). In this version, there is no sugar at all—just the sugar from the grape juice and the fruits. In the second variation, I decided to use sugar in all of its sweet glory and make a traditional berry cobbler. I was thrilled when everyone picked the fruit-sweetened version as their favorite! Was it because their palates had gotten used to desserts that are less sweet, or was it because the following recipe gets the balance of fruit and cobbler topping and juice sweetener just right? It's win-win either way. Don't omit the crème fraîche to serve alongside—its nutty creaminess goes perfectly with the tart sweetness of the berries.

1. Place a rack in the center of the oven and preheat to 350°F [175°C].

2. Using a stand mixer fitted with the paddle attachment (or with an electric hand mixer), briefly mix the 175 g/1¼ cups flour, baking powder, baking soda, ¼ tsp salt, and 2 tsp of the cinnamon on low speed until combined. Add the cold butter and beat on low speed for 30 to 45 seconds, or until the butter is broken down into pea-sized pieces or smaller. (Alternatively, use a pastry cutter or two knives to cut the butter into the dry ingredients; proceed as directed.)

SERVES

8 TO 10

3. In a small bowl, whisk together the egg yolks, 120 g/½ cup of the crème fraîche, and the vanilla until thoroughly mixed. With the mixer on low speed, pour the crème fraîche mixture into the flour-butter mixture and beat for 20 to 30 seconds, or until the dough comes together. (Or add the liquid all at once to the dry ingredients and use a wooden spoon to mix the wet and dry ingredients together.) It will be a bit shaggy like a biscuit dough. Wrap the dough loosely in plastic wrap and refrigerate while you make the filling.

4. In a small saucepan, bring the grape juice concentrate to a boil over medium-high heat, decrease the heat to medium-low, and simmer the juice for 10 to 15 minutes, or until it reduces to about 1 cup [240 ml]. It will get very thick and syrupy so be careful not to let it over-boil. To check to see if it is reduced enough, every now and then pour the juice into a measuring cup to measure it; if it is not 1 cup [240 ml], pour it back into the saucepan to continue to simmer and reduce until it measures out to 1 cup [240 ml]. Whisk in the room-temperature butter.

5. In a large bowl, toss the blueberries, raspberries, blackberries, and strawberries with the 45 g/ 5 Tbsp flour, remaining ¼ tsp cinnamon, and a pinch of salt until well coated. Add the juice syrup and lemon juice and mix gently to coat the fruit. Pour the fruit mixture into a 9-by-13-in [23-by-33-cm] baking pan. Remove the cobbler dough from the refrigerator and, using your hands, pinch off small, marble-sized pieces of dough and evenly distribute them on top of the berries. You won't be able to cover all of the berries, but that is okay. Brush the tops of the dough with the cream, allowing the extra cream to drip into the berries.

6. Bake the cobbler for 25 to 35 minutes, or until the cobbler dough is nicely browned and firm to the touch. Remove from the oven and let cool on a wire rack for 30 to 45 minutes. Serve the cobbler warm or at room temperature with generous dollops of the remaining crème fraîche. The cobbler can be stored, well wrapped with plastic wrap, in the refrigerator for up to 3 days. Bring to room temperature before serving, or warm in a 300°F [150°C] oven for 10 to 15 minutes.

ALMOND CREAM

- One 335-g/12-oz can frozen apple juice concentrate, thawed
- 50 g/½ cup almond flour
- 55 g/4 Tbsp unsalted butter, at room temperature
- 1 large egg
- 1 Tbsp all-purpose flour
- 1 tsp vanilla extract
- Pinch of kosher salt
- ⅛ tsp ground cinnamon

- 3 medium Empire, McIntosh, Golden Delicious, Gala, or other sweet baking apples, peeled, cored, and cut into ⅛-in [3-mm] slices
- 125 g/½ cup unsweetened applesauce
- 1 Tbsp vanilla extract
- ¼ tsp ground cinnamon
- ⅛ tsp freshly grated nutmeg
- Pâte Brisée (see page 88)
- 1 large egg
- 25 g/¼ cup sliced almonds

MAKES

ONE

9-IN [23-CM] CROSTATA

FRENCH APPLE-ALMOND CROSTATA

We live in apple country here in New England, and as soon as you start to feel a bit of chill in the morning air, thoughts go to apple picking and orchards and all of the marvelous things you can do with apples. We planned a Flour outing one year and everyone was instructed to fill—make that over-fill—their bag with apples, and we'd make something fun out of them all. By the end of the afternoon, we had each eaten at least three or four apples (okay, maybe I had five), and the thought of eating anything apple-y again made my stomach turn. Thankfully, by the next day my stomach rejuvenated, and I created this apple tart sweetened only by some reduced apple juice and a heaping pile of apples and almonds. It's quickly become my go-to recipe when I'm happily overrun with apples.

1. To make the almond cream: In a small saucepan, bring the apple juice concentrate to a boil over medium-high heat, decrease the heat to medium-low, and simmer for 15 to 25 minutes, or until the juice reduces to ¾ cup [180 ml]. It will thicken up slightly, become syrupy, and boil a little slower as it reduces. Watch out that it does not over-boil or burn; you may need to decrease the heat as it thickens. To check to see if it is reduced enough, every now and then pour the juice into a measuring cup to measure it; if it is not ¾ cup [180 ml], pour it back into the saucepan to continue to simmer and reduce until it measures out to ¾ cup [180 ml]. Remove from the heat, transfer to a bowl, and cool in the refrigerator until cold to the touch.

Continued

2. In a small bowl, using a wooden spoon, stir together the almond flour, butter, egg, all-purpose flour, vanilla, salt, cinnamon, and ¼ cup [60 ml] of the reduced apple juice (save the rest for later on in this recipe). Beat well until thoroughly combined. It may look a bit curdled but that is okay. The almond cream can be stored in an airtight container in the refrigerator for up to 1 week; bring to room temperature before using.

3. In a medium bowl, toss the apple slices with the remaining ½ cup [120 ml] reduced apple juice. In a small bowl, stir together the applesauce, vanilla, cinnamon, and nutmeg.Set both bowls aside.

4. Line a baking sheet with parchment paper.

5. On a well-floured work surface, roll out the pastry dough into a circle about 12 in [30 cm] in diameter. Transfer the dough circle to the prepared baking sheet. (You are going to assemble the crostata directly on the baking sheet so that you don't have to move it once it is finished to bake it.) Brush off any loose flour from the dough, and spread the almond cream evenly in the center of the dough in a circle about 7 in [18 cm] in diameter, leaving a border of about 2½ in [6 cm] of exposed dough all around. Spread the flavored applesauce evenly over the almond cream. Arrange the apple slices in concentric circles on top of the applesauce, layering and overlapping the slices on top of each other as needed to use all of the apples. Brush the tops of the apples with any leftover juice from the bowl. Starting at one side, fold up the exposed dough towards the center and then continue around the crostata, folding up the exposed dough toward the center, leaving the fruit exposed in the center and pleating the dough as you go to create a pretty free-form tart. Refrigerate the crostata, lightly covered with plastic wrap, for at least 1 hour or up to 1 day before baking to relax the dough.

6. Place a rack in the center of the oven and pre-heat to 350°F [175°C].

7. Crack the egg into a small bowl and whisk well; using a pastry brush, brush the egg wash all over the top of the pastry dough. Sprinkle the dough evenly with the almonds. Bake the crostata for 45 to 55 minutes, or until the dough is deep golden brown. Remove from the oven and let cool for 30 to 45 minutes on a wire rack. Cut into slices and serve. The crostata can be stored in an airtight container at room temperature for up to 2 days; for best eating, rewarm in a 300°F [150°C] oven for 10 to 12 minutes.

CARROT-PINEAPPLE CAKE
WITH CREAM CHEESE FROSTING

Flour is somewhat famous for its carrot cake. Or maybe it's just that it is my husband, Christopher's, most favorite Flour cake, so in my mind it's the most famous cake we have. Countless special occasions have been celebrated at the Chang-Myers household with a slice of carrot cake and two forks. (Yes, I suppose we could each get our own slice, but I always think the cake is going to be a present for Christopher and then I simply can't help but join in.)

So when it came time to try and develop a low-sugar—make that *no-sugar*—version of this cake, I knew I had my work cut out for me. Flour's carrot cake is decidedly one of the sweeter things we offer; the cake itself is sweet and the frosting has a fair amount of sugar in it as well. How could I get the same luscious, rich, addictive flavor without using any sugar? Could I create a cake that would be as good as the one that Christopher adores? It turns out that, using a few tricks up my sleeve, the answer is YES! Apple juice concentrate acts as the sweetener here along with pineapple juice that is reduced down until syrupy. The pineapple is naturally sweet, and two kinds of raisins help make your mind think this cake is laden with sugar. The frosting is a variation of a cream cheese frosting that my pastry chef Sarah used when making her own wedding cake. It's creamy, tangy, and lightly sweetened with more reduced apple juice. You'll feel good about making this cake for your family—and I feel great about bringing this home, not just for special occasions, but for every occasion.

Continued

CREAM CHEESE FROSTING

- One 335-g/12-oz can frozen apple juice concentrate, thawed
- 225 g/8 oz cream cheese, at room temperature
- 480 g/2 cups heavy cream
- ½ tsp ground cinnamon
- 2 tsp vanilla extract
- ⅛ tsp kosher salt

CARROT CAKE

- 75 g/¾ cup walnuts, coarsely chopped
- 120 g/¾ cup raisins
- 120 g/¾ cup sultanas (golden raisins)
- One 335-g/12-oz can frozen apple juice concentrate, thawed
- One 225-g/8-oz can pineapple chunks, in their own juices
- 4 large eggs
- 120 g/½ cup crème fraîche (see page 24)
- 120 g/½ cup whole milk
- 250 g/1¼ cups vegetable oil
- 1 Tbsp vanilla extract
- 315 g/2¼ cups all-purpose flour
- 2½ tsp baking powder
- ½ tsp baking soda
- ½ tsp kosher salt
- 1 Tbsp ground cinnamon
- 2 tsp ground ginger
- 1 tsp freshly grated nutmeg
- 130 g/1 cup tightly packed peeled and shredded carrots

- Fresh fruit or chopped, toasted walnuts for garnish

MAKES

ONE
DOUBLE-LAYER
8-IN [20-CM] CAKE

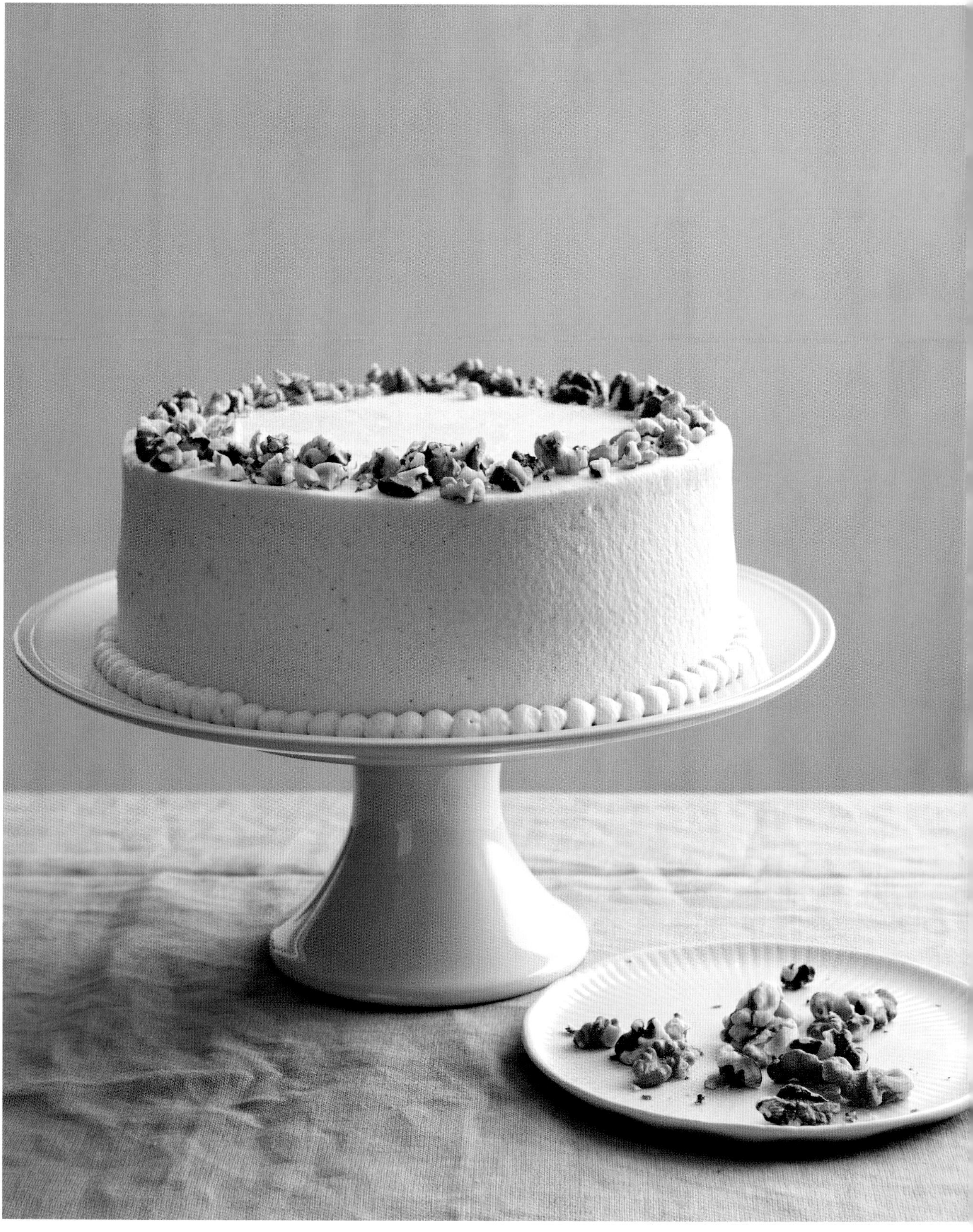

1. At least 4 hours in advance, make the frosting: In a small saucepan, bring the apple juice concentrate to a boil; decrease the heat to medium-low and simmer for 20 to 25 minutes, or until the juice reduces to ¾ cup [180 ml]. It will thicken up, become syrupy, and boil a little slower as it reduces. Watch out that it does not over-boil or burn; you may need to decrease the heat as it thickens. To check to see if it is reduced enough, every now and then pour the juice into a measuring cup to measure it; if it is not ¾ cup [180 ml], pour it back into the saucepan to continue to simmer and reduce until it measures out to ¾ cup [180 ml]. Remove from the heat, transfer from the pan into a bowl, and cool in the refrigerator until cold to the touch.

2. Using a stand mixer fitted with the whisk attachment (or an electric hand mixer), whip the cream cheese and ½ cup [120 ml] of the reduced apple juice concentrate on medium speed for 2 to 3 minutes, or until it is light and fluffy, scraping the bowl occasionally with a rubber spatula to get all of the cream cheese whipped up. (Reserve the rest of the apple juice for another use such as adding it to oatmeal or drizzling on ice cream, or discard.) Slowly drizzle in the cream and beat on medium speed for 1 to 2 minutes, or until the cream thickens and combines with the cream cheese mixture. Add the cinnamon, vanilla, and salt and mix until well combined. Scrape the frosting into an airtight container and refrigerate for at least 4 hours or up to 3 days. The frosting needs to firm up before you can use it. You will have about 4 cups [960 ml] of frosting.

3. To make the cake: Place a rack in the center of the oven and preheat to 350°F [175°C]. Butter and flour two 8-in [20-cm] round cake pans, or butter the pans and line the bottoms with parchment paper.

4. Put the walnuts on a baking sheet and toast for 8 to 10 minutes, or until lightly toasted. Set aside to cool.

5. Put the raisins and sultanas in a small bowl and pour hot water over to cover. Let sit for 30 minutes, then drain.

6. In a medium saucepan, combine the apple juice concentrate and the juice from the pineapple chunks. Chop the pineapple into small pieces and set aside in a bowl. Bring the juices to a boil over medium-high heat, decrease the heat to medium-low, and simmer for 20 to 25 minutes, or until the liquid reduces to ¾ cup [180 ml]. It will thicken up, become syrupy, and boil a little slower as it reduces. Watch out that it does not over-boil or burn; you may need to decrease the heat as it thickens. To check to see if it is reduced enough, every now and then pour the juice into a measuring cup to measure it; if it is not ¾ cup [180 ml], pour it back into the saucepan to continue to simmer and reduce until it measures out to ¾ cup [180 ml]. Remove from the heat, transfer to a bowl, and cool in the refrigerator until cold to the touch.

7. In a large bowl, whisk together the apple juice concentrate, eggs, crème fraîche, milk, vegetable oil, vanilla, and reserved chopped pineapple until well combined. In a medium bowl, stir together the flour, baking powder, baking soda, salt, cinnamon, ginger, nutmeg, carrots, raisins, sultanas, and walnuts. Add to the egg mixture and fold together with a rubber spatula until well combined.

Continued

8. Scrape the batter into the prepared pans, dividing equally. Bake for 35 to 45 minutes, or until the cakes are light brown (they won't color as much as a full-sugar cake) and spring back when you touch them in the center with your finger. They will not dome very much, if at all. Remove the cakes from the oven and let cool on a wire rack until you can pop them out of the pans. When the cakes are completely, totally cool (if they are at all warm, the frosting will melt off and it will be a mess), remove them from the pans. Using a long serrated knife, trim the tops of the cakes so they are level (they don't usually round too much but it's nice to level them off if they do). Place one cake on a plate or cake pedestal (use a cake turner if you have one), and spoon about 1 cup [240 ml] chilled frosting on top; using an offset spatula, spread the frosting evenly all the way to the edges of the cake.

9. Carefully place the second cake on top of the first cake (place it upside down so the even, sharp edges will be on the top of your finished cake), and spoon about 1 cup [240 ml] frosting on top. Spread the frosting thinly to the edges and down the sides of the cake, smoothing it as well as you can and covering the entire cake with a thin layer of frosting. This layer of frosting is called a crumb coat; it keeps loose crumbs from migrating to the surface of the finished cake. (At this point, it helps to refrigerate the cake for about 15 minutes to help set the crumb coat; it's not crucial but if you have time, it makes frosting a little easier.)

10. When you are done with the crumb coat, spoon a heaping 1 cup [240 ml] frosting on the cake and spread it evenly across the top and sides again. This is the final finishing layer of frosting. Fill a piping bag fitted with a small round tip with the remaining frosting, and pipe a border around the bottom of the cake, if you wish, or pile it on top of the cake.

11. The cake can be stored in an airtight container in the refrigerator for up to 2 days. Any longer than that and the frosting will get softer and may slide off of the cake. Remove the cake from the refrigerator 2 to 3 hours before serving, garnish with fresh fruit or chopped nuts, and serve the cake at cool room temperature.

KABOCHA SQUASH SPICE CAKE

- 1 small kabocha squash, quartered and seeded
- 160 g/⅔ cup pitted and finely chopped Medjool dates
- ½ tsp baking soda
- 1 vanilla bean
- 160 g/⅔ cup whole milk
- 100 g/½ cup vegetable oil, such as canola
- 1 Tbsp peeled and grated fresh ginger
- 2 large eggs
- 245 g/1¾ cups all-purpose flour
- 1½ tsp baking powder
- ½ tsp ground cinnamon
- ¼ tsp freshly grated nutmeg
- ¼ tsp kosher salt
- Unsweetened whipped cream or crème fraîche (see page 24) for garnish

When people ask me what I would have for my last meal, I always describe my favorite dishes my mom made while I was growing up: *mapo tofu*, noodle stir-fries, greens sautéed with something magical to make them the most delicious vegetables ever, pretty much anything she put on the table. I grew up eating amazing food, and I'm grateful to her for instilling in me an appreciation and passion for good eating. (Which is a very nice way of saying, "Thanks, Mom, for fueling my food obsession!") So when she was visiting a few years ago and told me about a new dish that she had to show me, I was all ears. We went to the Asian market and bought a hefty kabocha squash, also called Japanese pumpkin. While she was baking it, I went out and she had me fetch some Cheddar cheese and mayonnaise. She mixed the baked squash flesh with gobs of mayo and chunks of cheese and then put it under the broiler. It was about as unappetizing as it sounds. Sorry, Mom.

However, it wasn't a total fail because it did introduce me to the amazing kabocha squash. It's green with some orange flecks, is round like a pumpkin, and the flesh is incredibly creamy and sweet. I filed it away in my mind as something I'd want to play around with some day.

Here is the day! I made an unbelievable spice cake using the squash and some dates as the source of sweetener. The squash makes the cake incredibly moist, which can be an issue with no-sugar baked goods, and it takes especially well to these spices and vanilla.

1. Cut the quartered squash into large pieces, place in a medium saucepan, and fill with water to cover the squash. Bring the water to a boil over high heat, decrease the heat so that water simmers, and simmer for 30 to 40 minutes, or until the squash is tender and you can pierce it easily with a fork. Remove from the heat and let the squash cool in the water.

Continued

MAKES

ONE

8-IN [20-CM] CAKE

2. Put the dates and baking soda in a small bowl and add enough hot water to cover the dates. Stir to dissolve the baking soda; it will soften the skins of the dates, allowing them to blend more easily into the cake batter. Let the dates soak for 10 to 15 minutes. Drain the dates and mash them well with a fork to make a purée, and set aside.

3. Place a rack in the center of the oven and preheat to 350°F [175°C]. Butter and flour an 8-in [20-cm] round cake pan.

4. Remove the squash from the water, then mash the squash—skin and all—with a fork to make a coarse purée. Measure out 120 g/½ cup of the purée and reserve in a small bowl. Save any remaining squash purée for another purpose such as mixing into a stew or using as a sandwich spread.

5. With a paring knife, slit the vanilla bean lengthwise, and scrape out the seeds into a medium saucepan. Add the squash purée and the milk to the saucepan and stir with a wooden spoon to combine. Bring to a simmer over medium-low heat and cook gently for a few minutes until the squash completely mushes up in the milk and the vanilla seeds are well incorporated. Remove from the heat.

6. In a large bowl, whisk together the vegetable oil with the mashed dates and ginger until well combined. Add the squash purée and continue to whisk well. Add the eggs and whisk until well combined.

7. In a medium bowl, stir together the flour, baking powder, cinnamon, nutmeg, and salt. Add to the date mixture and mix just until barely mixed in.

8. Using a rubber spatula, scrape the batter into the prepared pan and bake for 35 to 45 minutes, or until the cake springs back when you press it in the center with your finger. Remove from the oven and let cool completely in the pan on a wire rack. Turn the spice cake out of the pan. Slice and serve with a dollop of unsweetened whipped cream or crème fraîche. The spice cake can be stored, well wrapped in plastic wrap, at room temperature for up to 2 days.

ACKNOWLEDGMENTS

The kitchen is my happy place. Whether I'm stressed or tired or just plain hungry, stepping in front of a whirring mixer, a hot oven, a container of flour, and a bin of sugar instantly centers me. I am grateful I am able to share that joy of baking with others through writing cookbooks. I am even more grateful to the team of people that have helped me do so.

Thank you to Nicole, my indomitable executive pastry chef, for keeping the bakery running smoothly while I was focused on writing this book, and to Jes, our pastry assistant, for her careful baking, note taking, and photo-shoot prepping.

Huge thanks to the kitchen team at Flour Fort Point for sharing their tight kitchen quarters with me and eating seemingly endless versions of not-quite-there treats. Thank you also to the entire teams of Flour and Myers+Chang; you do your jobs so seamlessly and well that it allowed me to step away and write this book. I'm lucky and I know it!

I had two invaluable testers, Keith Brooks and Sandy Warner, who painstakingly tested numerous variations of recipes each time with as much enthusiasm as the first time. Thank you Keith for coming back for more after testing recipes for *Flour, Too*, and thank you Sandy for introducing yourself to me many years ago at a book signing and generously offering up your time and talents. You both made grand impacts in the development of these recipes.

Thank you to the students at Cambridge Culinary who also lent their baking skills to this book and tested many of these recipes for me; it is always a gratifying experience working with passionate, eager students.

I feel awfully fortunate to work with the uber-talented team at Chronicle Books. Thank you to Bill LeBlond, Sarah Billingsley, and Lorena Jones for cheering me on, throwing me their full support, and guiding me through this book; to Peter and David for being the best marketing fan club an author could have; to Alice for taking the mishmash of recipes and pictures and making a glorious book, and to everyone else at Chronicle who lends their skills and talents to my books.

Everyone should be so lucky to have an agent like Stacey Glick. She must represent other people, but I would never know because she is always so 100 percent focused on helping me navigate through the behind-the-scenes, inner workings of getting a cookbook written. Thank you, Stacey.

Working with my photographer Joe De Leo was a fabulous experience, and I have such respect for his professionalism, attention to detail, and careful eye. Our stylist Molly Shuster was a delight, and if you're drooling over the pictures you can thank her for her meticulous food styling.

Thank you, Mom and Dad; many years ago I took a less-traveled path and you hardly blinked an eye (at least that's how we all like to remember it now), and you've given me more love, support, and encouragement than any one person should be allowed to have. That has truly made all the difference.

And the biggest, bestest, hugest, mostest thanks go to my husband, Christopher. Thank you for gamely trying every version of each and every pastry and always giving me your honest no-holds-barred feedback; for not giving me the stink-eye when I had to cancel plans and reroute trips to make time for this book; for editing every last word of the manuscript when you'd rather be watching the Golf Channel (baffling); and mostly for loving me so fully it takes my breath away. I love you MOST.

INDEX